MICHAEL MANSFIELD KC was called to the Bar in 1967 and became Queen's Counsel in 1989. Passionate about civil liberties and overturning miscarriages of justice, he represented clients from the Birmingham Six, the Guildford Four, the Tottenham Three, the Cardiff Three and the Bridgewater Four. He has fought for the Orgreave miners and for the families of victims of Bloody Sunday, Hillsborough, the *Marchioness*, Lockerbie and Grenfell, as well as for the parents of Stephen Lawrence.

Following the tragic death of his daughter by suicide in 2015, he and his wife, Yvette Greenway, set up the charity SOS to campaign for the provision of mental health support and suicide awareness. He has published several books, including his autobiography *Memoirs of a Radical Lawyer* (Bloomsbury, 2009).

In 2017, Michael celebrated 50 years at the Bar, but shows no sign of retiring – in fact, he recently launched a podcast series called The Two Heads with fellow barrister Lorna Hackett. He lives with Yvette in Warwickshire.

THE

POWER

IN THE

PEOPLE

THE

POWER

IN THE

PEOPLE

NOT THE PEOPLE
IN POWER

How We Can Change the World

MICHAEL MANSFIELD

monoray

First published in Great Britain in 2023 by Monoray,
an imprint of Octopus Publishing Group Ltd
Carmelite House
50 Victoria Embankment
London EC4Y 0DZ
www.octopusbooks.co.uk

An Hachette UK Company
www.hachette.co.uk

ISBN 978-1-80096-144-9

A CIP catalogue record for this book is available from the British Library.

Printed and bound in the UK.

1 3 5 7 9 10 8 6 4 2

Typeset in 11/16pt Plantin MT Pro by Jouve (UK), Milton Keynes.

This FSC® label means that materials used
for the product have been responsibly sourced.

In memory of Stéphane Hessel,
an outstanding international emissary for human
rights, whose life is detailed in Chapter 13.

A special dedication to my wife, Yvette Greenway,
who confronts adversity on a daily basis with
consummate courage and determination, and has
been a crucial inspiration for SOS.

Contents

Prologue
The Front Line in 1670

No matter where you are in the world, you will be familiar with the grasping, overweening, arrogant and often corrupt exercise of power by those whose sole object is to hang onto it. Lord Acton, the reputed 19th-century historian, famously encapsulated the process:

> Power tends to corrupt; absolute power
> corrupts absolutely.

There is, however, an antidote – the power in the people. This is their story. Hewn from the hard rock of lawfare. An insight into what it takes and why. A tribute to singular courage.

This book highlights the initiatives that often go without the attention and the acknowledgement they deserve. Such spirit is supposed to be the very fundament of our system of justice and is commemorated by a small plaque tucked away on the ground floor of the Central Criminal Court, the Old Bailey in London. Unless you stray into the further reaches of the oldest part of the building, you would never know the plaque was there, let alone understand what it represents.

It marks the spot where, around 350 years ago, trials took place involving citizens who stood by their principles, despite the railings and threats of the established order against their defiance, particularly by the presiding judge. All of this has a great resonance with what is going on as I write in 2023.

The plaque records the stalwart stance taken by the jury during the trial of two defendants – both Quakers – one of whom, William Penn, went on to found the American colony of Pennsylvania. The other, William Mead, a linen merchant, remained in Britain to assist George Fox, the founder of the Quakers.

Near this site
WILLIAM PENN and WILLIAM MEAD
were tried in 1670
for preaching to an unlawful assembly
in Grace Church Street
This tablet commemorates
The courage and endurance of the Jury Thos Vere,
Edward Bushell,

and ten others who refused to give a verdict
against them, although
locked up without food for two nights,
and were fined for their final
Verdict of Not Guilty

The case of these Jurymen was reviewed
on a writ of Habeas Corpus
and Chief Justice Vaughan delivered the opinion
of the Court
which established The Right of Juries to
give their Verdict
according to their Convictions

The case became the cornerstone for the independence
and primacy of the jury in our system of criminal
justice and established the part conscience plays in the
determination of verdict. In other words, the right of
conscientious objection. It is a central protection against
overweening and arbitrary power, which has angered
successive governments ever since.

It is, however, only half the story. The other half
concerns the legislation and trial of the two Quakers,
which perceptive readers will note bears a striking
resemblance to current events in the United Kingdom,
especially England.

After the death of Oliver Cromwell, there followed a period of restored monarchy, whereupon Parliament introduced a raft of oppressive legislation intended to curtail dissent and opposition. The principal target was the Quakers. It reached its height with the Conventicles statutes of 1664 and 1670, entitled 'An Act to prevent and suppress seditious Conventicles' (any religious assembly, other than Church of England).

The acts imposed a fine on anyone who attended a religious gathering of more than five people – five shillings for a first offence, ten for a second. Anyone who permitted their house to be used as a meeting house for such an assembly was liable to pay a fine of 20 shillings for a first offence and 40 for a second.

Mere attendance was enough, no matter what was said or done. This was a somewhat significant point, since the majority of Quaker gatherings were akin to prayer meetings and held in silence.

Both defendants pleaded not guilty. While they accepted their presence at the meeting in Grace Church Street, they challenged various aspects of the process. They argued that the indictment had no foundation in law. Where is the law that includes sedition, for which they were arrested? The indictment only alleged preaching to the people and drawing a tumultuous company. Both relied on their ancient liberties being invaded but were prevented by the judge from completing their defence before the jury.

Essentially, the judge directed the jury to convict 'without more'*, and ruled that they did not need to hear the defendants' rationale. The jury, however, refused to convict of unlawful assembly. This was not accepted by the judge, who threatened the jury that they would be locked up without sustenance of any kind – they faced the prospect of being starved into submission. This was their fate for two consecutive days and nights, yet on each day the jury returned the same verdict.

This was an inspiring and historic stand by ordinary citizens, in court, with defendants and jurors uniting against the might of the state. As we shall see, this pattern would continue to repeat itself, time and time again.

---

* 'Without more' is a phrase used by lawyers meaning you don't need more of anything, that is no more evidence nor argument.

Introduction
A Few Words on Power
and Change

The term 'power' has several connotations. When used to describe those 'in power' it evokes negative overtones linked to oppression and exploitation. Effectively it is concerned with power and control over others.

Power in people is quite different. It is not a faculty of control. It is the utilisation of an internal force. It is a capacity everyone has to influence the course of events and bring about change.

The perennial problem is converting this potential force in each of us into meaningful, realistic and effective actions, especially in circumstances where the odds seem to be insuperable. When pitted against the individual citizen, the power of those in authority can feel distinctly disempowering.

Change, however, is happening all around us.

Whether we like it or not, nothing stays precisely the same – in our own personal universe or in the astronomic one. Expanding, growing, moving, transcending, transforming . . . society is in a constant state of metamorphosis and mutation. Our own daily movements and encounters, however seemingly static, incrementally alter our relationships with others and with the environment that surrounds us. We may notice it in others more than we do in ourselves, but when we leave a room, in a sense, we are not the same person as we were when we entered it.

Human beings suffer a plethora of dramatic situations – flooding, war, extreme hunger and poverty, wildfires, drought, energy shortages, pandemics, climate change – and there is a strong human complicity in both the causes and the effects of all of them. So it's hardly surprising that, in the wake of such catastrophes, there is an opposite reaction, a very human and natural outcry – could this have been prevented or at least avoided?

It is at this point that citizens – ordinary people, those injured, the relatives of those killed – are committed to change for the benefit of future generations. Yet even though it has the power, the system rarely automatically corrects itself. Unless the people in power are held to account by the vigilance and pressure of the people most impacted, nothing will happen.

The individuals and groups of individuals written about in this book are among those people who have been driven by terrible circumstance to effect change. The true scale of their achievements is inspirational yet under-recognised. In many instances, it has taken decades of persistence, patience and pressure, exacerbated by hostility and indifference on the part of authority. Financial and emotional resources have regularly run down to the wire. And yet, against all the odds, it seems, they have achieved change.

A judge recently observed that there is a striking synonymity between the recent climate change protests and the suffragette and anti-apartheid movements. In May 2021, District Judge Bisgrove sitting at the City of London Magistrates' Court heard a case of obstruction during a mass Extinction Rebellion demonstration. Rowan Tilly, aged 63, was convicted of the charge, but sentenced to an 'absolute discharge', which means that he was not in practice penalised for that conviction. The judge cited anti-apartheid civil rights protests in America and South Africa, the suffragette movement and CND protests as having contributed to change.

The objectives of all these movements have been identical – truth to power, the accountability of power, and especially change in power and policy. Above all, no one wants future generations to suffer the same outcomes. It's not about money or compensation; it's about power being exercised responsibly and in the public, not the private, interest.

My career as a barrister has afforded me a front row seat to witness this shift of power. And while at times it might seem like the ordinary person is losing out against vested interests, corporations and power-hungry governments, what I have seen tells me that this is not in fact the case.

Despite the best efforts of the people in power, ultimately, it is the power in the people that swings it.

Occasionally this phenomenon erupts onto the world stage as an irresistible collective movement to bring down long-standing walls, remove regimes or challenge established preconceptions. But more often, at another level, the same force has the capacity to rectify iniquities and the injustice of the system, with far-reaching repercussions for all. It is important to recognise that these initiatives are momentous, even though on the ground, at the time, it is sometimes difficult to discern. They help to imbue governance with an element of democracy and accountability, sadly lacking in the people in power.

Chapter 1
Bluebottle

My own journey of exploration and revelation started with my mother, Marjorie, and her very straightforward response to a commonplace experience. Both my parents were glowing examples of post-WW2 citizens – honest, hardworking, God-fearing and above all, law-abiding citizens with entrenched Conservative views. So it was that we lived in Finchley, the electoral North London blue-rinse bedrock which, in 1959, propelled Margaret Thatcher to power as an MP.

To give you an idea of how this played out, once I hit my mid-teens, my dear mother felt she should prepare me for a world beyond Whetstone, the part of the Finchley constituency where we lived. Her idea for me to make the right friends, especially girls, was to learn to dance – quickstep and foxtrot. So off I went to a dance class in a cavernous room above the Red Lion pub in High Barnet. Her second idea was for me to join a tennis club, where

I might enjoy doubles. So off I went to join a club somewhere near Golders Green. Her final idea – la crème de la crème – was for me to join the Young Conservatives and partake of their super socials and proper dances. This one was a step too far for me, so to mollify my mother's anxiety, I had a rash rush to the head and volunteered to help her electioneering for the Tories. She had a voracious appetite for envelopes, which had to be filled with the latest exhortations to vote for . . . wait for it . . . Marjorie for Margaret!

My job was to hand deliver these envelopes. Just think – I could have changed the course of history had I dumped them in the local Dollis Brook. Instead, I have a letter of gratitude from the first woman Prime Minister – Mrs Thatcher – addressed to my mother ('Dear Mrs Mansfield . . .'), something that has caused a degree of consternation among those who have viewed me as a 'red under the bed'.

My father had 'lost a leg', as he amusingly put it, while serving in a mounted division of the City of London Yeomanry in the Middle East during WW1. This meant he was unable to drive a car. In the late 1950s, we had an early version of the 'sit up and beg' Ford Anglia and my mother did all the driving. She had driven ambulances as a member of the Air Raid Precautions in London during the Blitz and also driven my father regularly by night across North London in the blackout, navigating only using the cats' eyes in the middle of the road, to his emergency railway work as a controller in Uxbridge. She was consequently a proficient and careful driver.

In the years after the war, rationing and austerity impacted every family. My mother made everything last as long as possible. We had one joint of meat each week, which was judiciously apportioned every day. She bought the joint at the same time every Thursday from a small branch of Sainsbury's on the High Road. She parked the car in the same place outside, where there were no meters nor yellow lines.

But then came the day when a summons appeared in the post, alleging she had parked between the studs of a pedestrian crossing near to Sainsbury's.

Marjorie was having none of this. Her indignation was incandescent and could be felt the length and breadth of the road on which we lived. Against everyone's advice, at a time when officers in the Metropolitan Police were fit for purpose (or so it was firmly believed), Mrs Marjorie Mansfield of 73 Naylor Rd, London N20, decided to challenge the allegation and face a Magistrates' Court hearing. Not only that, also against everyone's advice, she decided to defend herself.

I still fondly imagine her in a long beige overcoat, gloves and a sturdy black handbag in hand, going into battle, inspired by the legend attached to where we lived – the

'Whetstone' our neighbourhood was named for was used by soldiers to sharpen their swords before the Battle of Barnet in 1471!

The day of judgement arrived. She took her place alongside the usual parade of petty criminals.

A rare sight no doubt for the bench. The officer who had summonsed her must have thought the whole thing was a bit of a curiosity and a formality and he maintained his version of this quite simple violation.

My mother, however – upright, without a single blemish on her record, let alone a previous conviction – was equally immovable. Never in a month of Sundays (even though it was a Thursday) would she commit an offence against any law, at any time, or in any place. But unbeknown to the officer, and in true Perry Mason style, she had an evidential Exocet missile – my father!

The officer had plainly not looked beyond the end of his nose. On the day in question, my disabled father had been sitting, as he customarily did, in the front passenger seat of the car, closest to the pavement. In court, he confirmed in the clearest terms that there were no studs within sight.

The result? A resounding acquittal: unheard of, I guess, back then. It even found its way into the local newspaper. My mother, an upstanding woman of the Conservative community, had defended herself against injustice – and won!

The fallout for me was long term. Thereafter, whenever we ventured forth in the car, if my mother spotted a police officer, she would raise her voice pointedly, 'There's one, over there!' Sitting in the back seat, I even devised an *I Spy* book for her. And she would recount the story again, wondering what lies were being contrived by this member of the force – because if they could do that to her, just in relation to parking, what on earth would they get up to in relation to more serious crime? She warned me never to believe a man in uniform. From then on, they were called 'bluebottles' in our house.

This one incident had undermined her faith in authority forever and got me thinking. I'm not sure she realised the lasting effect it would have on me. Had she done so, and witnessed the kind of work I've ended up doing over the last forty years, she might have had second thoughts.

Chapter 2
Awakening

When I was called to the Bar in November 1967, the British judicial system was heralded on the world stage as an example of the gold standard in fairness, due process and intellectual rigour.

This image was reinforced by the contributions made by English judicial luminaries in the post-war years to the Nuremberg trials of German war criminals and to the legal framework of the European Convention on Human Rights (ECHR), within which it might be possible to prevent future atrocities.

This reputation, however, masked a somewhat different picture on the ground, where prejudice, the presumptions of class and assumptions of guilt were written into the fabric of daily justice. Outcomes were couched in resigned acceptance and deep-seated deference.

Uncovering the fallibilities was not (and never has been) brought about by failsafe processes within the system itself. The habitual reaction of the powers that be, when faced with shortcomings, is invariably one of denial. The system was projected as being as close to perfection as is humanly possible. The difficulty of dismantling this façade was graphically described by Ludovic Kennedy in his book *Ten Rillington Place* about the wrongful murder conviction of Timothy Evans, tried and hanged in 1950. Not only a book but also a celebrated film, it portrays the obduracy of established judicial thinking.

After my mother's experience, the book provided a spur to action. It was published in 1961, my first year at university, and gave me a purpose for the intellectual rigours of the philosophy degree course I had just started. To my unexpected pleasure and privilege, much later I would have the opportunity to meet Ludo during the Birmingham Six appeals and remain a friend until his death in 2009.

Public inquiries of any magnitude were certainly not a feature of the early years of my practice. They have evolved into what they are today because the public and, in particular, the families and friends of victims, have demanded answers to fundamental questions. Today we ask, How was it allowed to happen? Who was responsible? Who knew or should have known? And, How can it be prevented from happening again?

According to the Institute for Government, between 1960 and 1990 there were only 19 public inquiries, with none at all in some years. This compares to 69 public inquiries between 1990 and 2017, with never fewer than 3, and up to 16, running at any one time. Today, in the spring of 2023, there are several historic inquiries taking place: Infected Blood, Undercover Policing, Covid, the Manchester Arena bombing, the Salisbury novichok poisonings, Post Office Horizon IT, the Omagh bombing and the unlawful killings in Afghanistan. There is also the more recent Grenfell Tower Inquiry, which is ongoing.

The call for a public inquiry has today become the vital first response in the wake of serious systemic injustice or, more obviously, catastrophic disaster. The citizen has come to realise that an inquiry, if carried out expeditiously, is one of the few ways to achieve an element of truth and democratic accountability.

It is by no means the panacea for all ills, but it has helped to activate the public conscience and stimulate the individual spirit. This gradual awakening, which ran parallel to my early career, came about incrementally and imperceptibly, galvanised by voices in the wilderness which raised the alarm and ensured their message gradually percolated through and penetrated the bastions of convention. As a result, the culture of deference to what you are told by your so-called 'elders and betters' has given way to a healthy sense of scepticism and enduring environment of enquiry. This has happened to such an extent, now, that any assurance uttered by authority is rarely accorded little more than the value of the paper upon which it is written.

Inquiries often reveal that the system is demonstrably fallible. Glaring mistakes and misdemeanours are unravelled and exposed. Not by the efforts of any government treading the path of truth, but rather by those closest to the truth. In the well-worn words of a laundry powder commercial in the early 1970s, no longer can the system 'be held up to the light without a stain in sight!' It's time to change the machine, not just the powder!

This process of enlightenment and empowerment became a critical force behind reversing the notorious 'miscarriage of justice' cases of the 1970s and 1980s, and provoking legislative reform. For example, the Police and Criminal Evidence Act of 1984 created codes of practice intended to protect the rights of citizens, as balanced against the power of the police. This was followed by establishing a new process to deal with 'miscarriages' of justice, called the Criminal Cases Review Commission, an independent body set up to examine criminal convictions and sentences, rather than this being done by the Home Secretary.

At the same time, this internal force fuelled the Black community movement of resistance against bigotry and oppression within the system as a whole (which we will see through the Mangrove trials in Chapter 3, and later the case of Stephen Lawrence). Their struggle centred and depended on the courage and vision of individual citizens and their supporters, those who were not prepared any longer to put up with passive patient acquiescence as the only way out, but instead expended endless energy wringing change from a reluctant and obstructive authority. In many instances, the efforts of the Black community have been recognised and aided by committed investigative journalists who have broadcast the iniquities, much to the chagrin of some members of the senior judiciary.

But it's not all about big headlines and famous cases. Many incidents and cases go unseen, unheard, unheralded, despite being of equal stature and significance in the drive for change. I would like to start with one of these cases, which, as it happens, spans the whole period covered in this book.

Unheard – Mahmood Mattan

In September 1952, a lone figure of undoubted innocence faced the notorious state executioner Albert Pierrepoint. The condemned man was a Somali seaman and father of three, Mahmood Mattan. He was hanged in Cardiff prison for a crime he did not commit. It was to be the last execution at that prison.

At the time of Mahmood's death, I was ten years old. Another 57 years would pass before I played a part in redressing this iniquity.

The callous murder of Lily Volpert (41, and herself from an immigrant Ukrainian family) took place on the evening of 6 March 1952, inside her well-established shop in Bute Street, Cardiff. Her throat was cut with a razor from just below the chin up to the right ear and she suffered four other non-fatal cuts before bleeding to death. Lily lived on the premises with her sister and would usually shut up the shop at around 8pm, although she would also serve latecomers after that time. Her takings of the day – £100 – were stolen. The murder was not witnessed by anyone and did not give rise to any scientific traces.

The only lead the police had was a passing witness called Harold Cover. The first statement Cover gave to the police was taken the day after the murder. He described seeing two Somali men – one was standing against the shop window and the other was coming out of the doorway. The latter had a gold tooth and was not wearing a hat; Cover claimed to know him. He did not name anyone at that stage and, critically, Mahmood did not have a gold tooth.

The naming of Mahmood only arose once Cover became aware of a substantial financial reward offered by the victim's family. At the trial, Cover claimed to have seen Mahmood coming out of the porch of the shop, even though this account differed substantially from his initial statement. This claim would form the basis of Mahmood's conviction, although Cover was not a credible witness as the police well knew at the time.

Astonishing even by the rules of the day, this first statement was not disclosed to the defence but must have been known to the police. Additionally, the defence were not aware of four people who were in the vicinity of the shop at the time and who were asked to attend an identity parade – these four people either did not identify Mahmood or, in one case, explicitly said it was not him.

There was no one there for Mahmood at his hanging. His wife, Laura, only discovered her husband's fate when she turned up at the prison to find a notice pinned to the gates informing the public of the execution. Laura had faced a struggle from the off. She was 17 when she fell in love with Mahmood, not something her family or her community welcomed. Such was the prejudice and bigotry in 1952 that Mahmood, when he returned from seafaring work, had to live apart from Laura and their three sons, literally in the same road but on the other side in digs. The depth of this jaundiced predisposition can be judged from the way his own defence counsel depicted him to the jury at his trial: 'half child of nature, half semi-civilised savage'.

At the time of his execution, barely two months had passed since the conviction and a failed appeal, and only six months since the murder itself. An unvarnished race to the gallows.

These shocking events attracted little attention at the time and left Laura to face the lonely prospect of fighting overwhelming prejudice to clear her husband's name and establish the fact he had been 'killed by injustice' (the indelible words engraved on his gravestone).

Unknown to Laura and almost at the same time, another miscarriage of justice had unfolded with the wrongful execution in 1950 of another Welshman, Timothy Evans, for the murder of his daughter at 10 Rillington Place in London. Both Evans and the address were to become household names because of the involvement of the notorious serial killer 'Dr' John Christie. Christie admitted that Evans's wife was among his eight victims, but not Evans's daughter.

The task of finally clearing the name of Timothy Evans became associated with the legendary investigative journalist Ludovic Kennedy (mentioned above), who went on to play a significant role in pursuing later miscarriages of justice, such as the Birmingham Six.

Laura would, in the end, achieve for Mahmood what Ludo did for Timothy Evans: vindication for the individual dead, but more generally a significant contribution to the prospect of change – namely, the abolition of capital punishment and the introduction of a novel institutional power of scrutiny and vigilance within the system – the Criminal Cases Review Commission.

Laura's fight entailed battling hostility, which intensified with the stigma of the conviction and execution. Laura remained in Cardiff and kept her name, but tried to shield the children by explaining their father's absence by his work away as a merchant seaman. This bubble was burst by cruel abuse shouted in public at one of the children. From then on, the lives of all three children – David, Omar and Mervyn – were severely impacted, continuing right through to the present day and their own children. For Omar it was all too much and, as if in a gesture of remembrance in 2003, he was found alone and dead by the sea on a remote Scottish beach.

Whatever the pain and anguish, Laura held on to her belief in Mahmood's innocence. Unshaken, she fought to have his body exhumed from the prison and placed in the Muslim section of the Western Cemetery in Cardiff in 1996. The following year, when Laura was 67, she approached the Criminal Cases Review Commission (CCRC) to request their help to reopen the case. She had tried to get this done once before in 1969 by applying to the Home Secretary James Callaghan but her request had been rejected.

Lynette, partner of the late Mervyn Mattan, said, 'The case had been dormant in the 1980s, but when it was covered in the *South Wales Echo* we secured the solicitor Bernard de Maid, who said he would take the case for free. It was a last chance; the family were very much united in that effort.'

This time, in 1998*, Laura and her family's enduring efforts were finally rewarded. Mattan was the first case the newly formed CCRC referred successfully to the Court of Appeal. Bernard had instructed me to present the appeal and the preparation was painstaking but also dramatic.

One explosive revelation – something rarely experienced in real life – came virtually at the doors of the court. A final check on documents retained by police was being made by a colleague of mine, who was my junior on the appeal. Almost by accident, Anne Shamash stumbled across a note

---

*   This was the same year as the inquiry into the murder of Stephen Lawrence.

which bore feint handwriting. It was the hand of the senior investigating officer, DI Roberts, by then deceased:

The man seen by Cover was traced – Gass (Taher) and useless? Cover left Cory's Rest at 7.50pm, identifies the Somali in the porch as Gass.

Rapidly the jigsaw pieces fell into place. It was discovered that indeed a man named Gass had been spoken to four days after the murder, and confirmed not only that he lived in Bute Street but had passed the shop that evening and visited it earlier in the afternoon. In 1954, he was traced in relation to a murder by stabbing, deemed insane at his trial, committed to Broadmoor and ultimately deported to Somalia.

The final nadir in this appalling saga also occurred in the last days before the appeal. A telex circulated in the manhunt for Gass in 1954 was disclosed. It closed the circle:

A seaman born in British Somaliland 1920 5ft 7ins slim build black hair brown eyes dark complexion, a man of colour, gold tooth left upper jaw has been convicted of violence.

It was the gold tooth that completed the circle of guilt around Gass, and not Mahmood.

Technically, when the Court of Appeal quashes a conviction, it is not equivalent to an acquittal. It is merely determining that the conviction is not safe, for whatever reason. But here as a matter of obvious inference, the features of the real culprit had been recorded at the start – and it was not Mahmood.

The Crown conceded. The family, after many tense years of waiting, were able to witness the Court of Appeal quash the conviction with strong words that rang out loud and clear at the end of the judgement:

'It is a matter of profound regret that in 1952 Mahmood Mattan was convicted and hanged and that it has taken 46 years for that conviction to be shown to be unsafe. The Court can only hope that its decision today will provide some crumb of comfort for his surviving relatives. The case has a wider significance in that it clearly demonstrates five matters:

1. Capital punishment was not perhaps a prudent culmination for a criminal justice system which is human and therefore fallible.
2. In important areas, to some of which we have alluded, criminal law and practice have, since Mattan was tried, undergone major changes for the better.

3. The CCRC is a necessary and welcome body, without whose work the injustice in this case might never have been identified.
4. No one associated with the criminal justice system can afford to be complacent.
5. Injustice of this kind can only be avoided if all concerned in the investigation of crime, and the preparation and presentation of criminal prosecutions, observe the very highest standards of integrity, conscientiousness and professional skill.'

Surely this was a landmark in the annals of judicial utterances? Points 1 and 5 are the most telling. Point 1 should be remembered every time the 'hang 'em and flog 'em brigade' is on the march; and Point 5 every time the forces of law and order are found to be seriously compromised*.

For me, these observations in the context of a court hearing conjured up the horror and unbelievable tension there must have been for counsel defending in a capital

---

* This was relevant in 2022 when the Metropolitan Police was declared unfit for purpose in tackling corruption within its ranks, and again in 2023 when Baroness Casey's report declared the force institutionally racist for a second time, not to mention sexist, misogynistic and homophobic.

murder case. Thankfully, this was an experience I had missed as the death sentence was abolished just two years before I was called to the Bar. For Mahmood's family, however, and for Laura especially, these fears had been real and could not be dispelled.

The shocking and stark truth underpinning the case against Mahmood was not a mere matter of human error or oversight. It was the result of corrupted policing and racism. Luke, Mattan's grandson, said, 'How could I have faith in the criminal justice system for instance, and I'm afraid to say even the police. Since a young age I've always looked at them in a negative light. Because of what I've been told from young of what happened to my grandfather.'

Laura had finally reached the goal she had been aiming at for decades, but establishing the truth was only part of her objective. Accountability remained outstanding. Recognition and acceptance by those responsible might be a step in the right direction. Laura died on New Year's Day 2008, aged 78, but this ambition lived on in the heart of her family.

It was the 70th anniversary of Mahmood's execution in the summer of 2022, an event that spurred the conscience of the police authority, particularly when they realised that BBC Wales was about to run a compelling and graphic podcast series based on careful new research by the presenter Danielle Fahiya, entitled Mattan: Injustice of a Hanged Man. 'The BBC was told that the family would be receiving an apology,' explains Lynette. 'It was sent to the BBC with no real time to process it – 24 hours. It felt like an afterthought.'

The Chief Constable of South Wales Police, Jeremy Vaughan, issued a long-overdue apology, which was in the following terms:

There is no doubt that Mahmood Mattan was the victim of a miscarriage of justice as a result of a flawed prosecution, of which policing was clearly a part. This is a case very much of its time – racism, bias and prejudice would have been prevalent throughout society, including the criminal justice system. It is right and proper that an apology is made on behalf of policing for what went so badly wrong in this case 70 years ago and for the terrible suffering of Mr Mattan's family and all those affected by this tragedy for many years. Even to this day we are still working hard to ensure that racism and prejudice are eradicated from society and policing.

These fine words should not be scorned; better late than never. However, it is not what is said but what is not said that matters. It highlights the basic intransigence of entrenched power, which was tirelessly challenged by Laura and others like her who followed. There was not a word about why there has been such a massive and inexplicable delay in acceptance. It tends to suggest a chronic form of institutional denial and a deep-seated reluctance to come to terms with core deficiencies.

Natasha Grech, granddaughter of Mattan, said:

'I don't feel that this apology is directed towards the family at all. I feel that it's been quickly written and put out there on the back of the podcast. They've acknowledged, now, that it's been spoken out loud that there was not an apology, and I just feel that it's been, *get this written, get it out as quick as we can so that the family can't keep saying, "We've not had an apology, we want an apology"*. I don't feel it's heartfelt; I don't feel that it's worth the paper it's written on, if I'm being totally honest. It was not given to any of the family. You know, we are human beings, we have feelings. It would have been nice to have seen a police officer, maybe. It would have been nice to have been approached as a family.'*

---

* Time code 31.18 Natasha Grech – Granddaughter Episode 9 *Mattan: Injustice of a Hanged Man https://www.bbc.co.uk/sounds/play/p0df9zk1*

The focus of the statement is racism and prejudice – undoubted factors – in the hope that the attention will be deflected from the underlying malaise, which is surely an abject lack of integrity or, put bluntly in other words, dishonesty. There is within the statement not a word that acknowledges this, nor even an oblique reference.

Perhaps none of this is surprising when you learn that two other major Cardiff-based murder convictions, handled by subsequent generations of South Wales police from the late 1980s, were also overturned. The Cardiff Five then Three[*] and the Cardiff Newsagent Three[†] cases were

---

[*] Five innocent Black men were wrongly accused of the murder of Lynette White, a sex worker, in 1988. The investigation was characterised by oppressive questioning, unreliable confessions and fellow worker witnesses committing perjury, under duress from the police. Two of the men were acquitted at trial, and the convictions of the other three were overturned on appeal in 1992. Thirteen police officers stood trial, accused of 'moulding, manipulating, influencing and fabricating evidence', but the trial was terminated over matters of non-disclosure. Eventually, a single white culprit was traced through DNA and pleaded guilty in 2003.

[†] Three men were wrongly accused of the 1987 murder of Cardiff newsagent Phillip Saunders, who was attacked with a shovel outside his home and died later in hospital. After a police investigation based on unreliable confessions, coercive questioning and pressured witnesses, they were convicted of the crime in 1988. Their convictions were quashed on appeal in 1999.

both underpinned by suspect policing, as well as racism in the case of the former. Both required the force of family campaigns to undo these injustices. In both instances, it was ordinary people who finally set things straight, despite the very best efforts of the people in power.

Luke Mattan said:

'I see my grandfather's name as a symbol of strength as well as a symbol of injustice. Strength because of how he conducted himself by holding his head up high right to the last moment. Injustice because of the life that was taken away from him when he was an innocent man. My father always told me from young that my name is Luke Mattan and my grandfather was the last man who was innocently hung in HMP Cardiff.'[*]

Gathering Storm

The steady drops falling from the Mahmood case coincided with a much bigger, more publicised cloud cluster of cases which blew apart any vestige of reliable justice. In each one, the driving force for exposure and change was coming from the victims and their families.

---

*   Time code 33.52 Luke Mattan – Grandson Episode 9 *Mattan: Injustice of a Hanged Man https://www.bbc.co.uk/sounds/play/p0df9zk1*

The ones identified here are but the tip of the iceberg, and they are remembered notoriously by a number suffix: the Cardiff Five then Three; the Guildford Four; the Birmingham Six[*]; the Tottenham Three[†]; the Bridgewater Four[‡]. In each instance, defendants were wrongly convicted. The detail of the cases is elaborated upon in my memoirs[§]; here I am merely attempting to extrapolate the general themes of each as a backcloth to the struggle faced by those seeking truth.

In each of these cases, there are stark common factors which mirror what happened to Mahmood. Trials for horrific events surrounded by resultant hostility; racial prejudice – anti-Irish and black – towards the defendants; corrupt, dishonest and oppressive policing; convictions followed by failed initial appeals and applications.

---

[*] The Guildford Four and Birmingham Six cases both involved pub bombings in 1974, carried out as part of a campaign by the IRA (the Irish Republican Army) against British rule in the North of Ireland (the term used by those Republicans supporting a United Ireland).

[†] The Tottenham case concerned serious disturbances in 1985 on the Broadwater Farm Estate in London, during which PC Keith Blakelock was killed.

[‡] Carl Bridgewater was a 13-year-old newspaper boy shot at close range by men he stumbled across during a burglary in 1978.

[§] *Memoirs of a Radical Lawyer*, Michael Mansfield, Bloomsbury (2010).

Awakening the soul of justice in these circumstances was often a monumental task. A deal of persuading and canvassing and cajoling had to take place with a sceptical audience far removed from the current frame of mind. It was achieved in each instance by the persistence, strength and integrity of the victims, their friends and families, and the campaign collective. This was no easy matter when the majority were incarcerated and there were scant resources to sustain the research work, let alone the welfare of everyone involved.

This did not prevent prison rooftop protests and other events, but the real game-changer was the advent of investigative journalism into these miscarriages. Besides outstanding journalists like Paul Foot and Ludovic Kennedy, there were admirable television series, such as *World in Action*, *Trial and Error* and *Rough Justice*. The production companies behind them had the resources to trace witnesses, search documents, commission research and conduct experiments at a time when the CCRC had not yet come into existence. In this way, they could facilitate the groundwork for appeals via the Home Secretary and, in many cases, kick-start the whole process.

Of the cases identified above, a prime example was the Birmingham Six, who spent 16 years in jail for a crime they did not commit – the devastating IRA pub bombings in Birmingham in November 1974. Twenty-one people were killed and 182 injured in two huge explosions at two public houses. An unexploded device was found at a third. It was the worst atrocity since W W 2. Five men were arrested the same evening, having boarded a train from Birmingham to Heysham for a ferry to Northern Ireland, and a sixth was arrested in Birmingham. The case against them rested upon forensic science, explosive trace evidence and confessions. At their trial in 1975, all six were convicted and their first appeal was rejected in 1976.

Subsequently, anti-Irish feeling was at an all-time high, with openly hostile demonstrations in Birmingham. Overcoming the animosity and overturning convictions for a crime of this magnitude took extraordinary fortitude and stamina by the six men, who had been subject to violent and oppressive interrogation and doubtful science. They never hesitated nor gave up their hope that truth would prevail.

Over a decade passed before I became involved. I was instructed by Gareth Peirce, whose intrepid, caring and painstaking attention to detail carried the day. The six men were distinctively different personalities – for example, I found Paddy Hill fast-talking and ebullient, while Billy Power was quieter and more considered. They campaigned relentlessly from the confines of their tiny cells, so visiting was a whirlwind of discussion, turning over every forensic stone. Hugh Callaghan, who was retiring and courteous at all times, sadly died during the writing of this book.

Upon their original arrests in 1974, swabs were taken from the hands of the defendants for the purpose of detecting the presence of explosive traces (nitroglycerine). The test used was a basic presumptive field test called a Griess test. The swabs from two of the arrestees were positive. The Crown's expert, Dr Skuse, claimed that he was 99 per cent certain that such a result meant the person had handled nitroglycerine, and the subsequent convictions in 1975 very much hinged on this evidence.

Over the years, high-profile and insistent campaigning by the families caught the interest of assiduous journalists such as Charles Tremayne, Ian McBride and Chris Mullin*. They worked for Granada's *World in Action* in 1985 and undertook a complete reappraisal of the whole case, tracking the purported actual IRA perpetrators of the bombings in Ireland.

In passing, it is worth noting that some other sectors of the media, the *Sun* newspaper in particular, were highly derogatory about Chris Mullin – 'Loony MP backs bomb gang' and 'If the Sun had its way, we would have been tempted to string 'em up years ago.'

---

*   Chris Mullin later became a Member of Parliament and author, renowned for his seminal 1986 book on the bombings *Error of Judgement*.

A central part of the campaigning revolved around the reliability of the forensic tests. Could they have been spurious or false positives, caused by a substance other than nitroglycerine? Well-known and highly reputable scientists were engaged on behalf of the six men – funded at the outset by Granada – David Baldock, former head of the Home Office forensic laboratories in Nottingham, and Dr Brian Caddy, head of the Forensic Science Unit at Strathclyde University.

It was important to discover what the two men with 'positive' results had been doing and handling before they were arrested. Mr Baldock discovered that a number of disparate surfaces gave rise to positive results: nitrocellulose aerosol spray, chips and lacquer. Dr Caddy likewise. A cigarette packet, a varnished wood surface and two old packs of playing cards were shown to produce positive results in a Griess test. Further experiments with playing cards provided confirmation. This was important as the men had been playing cards on the train journey before they were arrested.

There was much else wrong with the science and with the interrogations in police custody. Overturning the convictions, however, remained a tortuous road. Famously, in 1980, Lord Denning prevented the men from pursuing a civil claim for damages for assault by the police, which he characterised as an 'appalling vista' – namely the idea that convicted terrorists could sue the police, attacking their credibility. Thereafter, Lord Chief Justice Lord Lane rejected their second appeal in 1988, playing down the importance of forensic evidence.

More meetings, more letters and more articles were necessary at a time of despair and despondency. Both strength and staunch belief were summoned from inside prison cells and at regular family and supporter gatherings in the community – until March 1991, when the Court of Appeal finally quashed the convictions. There were hugely jubilant scenes outside the Old Bailey where traffic, pedestrians and local construction workers stopped to applaud.

Paddy Hill, one of the six, was later to reflect in a BBC HARDtalk interview, 'The one thing about the British public – when they see an injustice they are not afraid to stand up and scream about it – and thank God.'

The cumulative effect of these miscarriage of justice cases and their associated campaigns was to finally force legislative change and radical reappraisal by the authorities. New safeguards and conditions were set for police interrogation and investigation, ensuring contemporaneous audio and visual recording and independent advice. There ensued a root-and-branch reappraisal of the criminal justice system as a whole – the Royal Commission on Criminal Justice under Viscount

Runciman. It was established in 1991 and reported in 1993. I provided my experiences to Professor Michael Zander KC, one of the members of the Commission.

The report's recommendations led to the Criminal Appeal Act 1995, which simplified the test for criminal appeals and, at the same time, established the Criminal Cases Review Commission. This replaced a haphazard and arbitrary process of appeal via the Home Secretary and was first used in the Mattan case, as I mentioned above.

This dark period of judicial history, therefore, ultimately spawned major reformative changes. The most far-reaching led to the demise of unreliable confessions – and hence convictions – that had been based on either fabrication or oppression.

Chapter 3
Thunder on the Streets

So far, I have given examples of iniquities and inequalities, mainly within the criminal justice system, which have been fought by stalwart individuals and groups of committed supporters who shifted the boundaries. There was, however, during these same years, an even wider and more tangible atmosphere of dissatisfaction about the absence of social justice. This surfaced in the form of movements challenging the customary precepts and gained its strength from collective public participation.

Although labels became attached to each of these movements, this was for the convenience of reference and did not mean they were homogeneous. Within them there were divisions of opinion and a variety of hues. The main thrust of each, however, was to empower, to activate, to demonstrate and to facilitate a feeling – to be able.

The Female Eunuch by Germaine Greer was published in 1970 and heralded the radical feminist movement.

Along with many others, I remember buying a copy, from a bookseller in the Charing Cross Road. I had, a few years before and much to everyone's amazement (including my own), successfully obtained a dual honours degree in Philosophy from Keele, a new university with a new vision, located on the edge of the potteries in Staffordshire.

The combination of its location, student politics and a truly challenging subject taught by a leading empiricist of his day, Professor Antony Flew, quickly replaced the fancies of Finchley. Semantic analysis and the works of David Hume took over and I was propelled into intellectual realms I had never heard of – Libertarianism, Anarchism and the Situationist movement in France. Greer's dissection of current thinking did not come as a shock to me.

Accepted and long-hallowed beliefs, centring on a fundamentally patriarchal society, were stripped away to uncover the biased structures that underpin our institutions. Slowly, the inbuilt disadvantages for women were exposed. It was a breath of fresh air which has maintained its essence for present-day voices in the MeToo revelations.

The Peace Movement, likewise, gained attention well beyond a simple anti-war message. It embraced a whole culture of non-violence, inspired by Mahatma Gandhi and his civil rights resistance to British governance. As Gandhi himself proclaimed and prophesied, 'There are many causes I am prepared to die for, but no causes I am prepared to kill for'.

This philosophy of peaceful mass civil protest became a cornerstone for CND, the Campaign for Nuclear Disarmament. At the end of WW2, in August 1945, hundreds of thousands of Japanese citizens were killed and maimed by nuclear bombs dropped on Hiroshima and Nagasaki. Three years later, the United Kingdom announced a programme for the development of its own nuclear weapons.

The first UK test took place on 3 October 1952, a month after the execution of Mahmood Mattan. Although the Australian Montebello Islands in the Pacific were uninhabited, the health of many perfectly fit British service personnel was severely affected by the tests – radiation, cancers, infertility, birth defects and musculoskeletal deficiencies resulted. Of the estimated 22,000* servicemen and women involved in the 11-year programme, about

---

* This massive exercise in the Pacific was spread across five locations and eleven years (1952–63), and involved 21,357 service personnel from the UK and another 8,000 from Australia. It's likely that some were security personnel, some were involved in maintenance and supplies, some protection, some armaments – and some were rumoured to be used unknowingly as guinea pigs to detect detrimental effects on the human body. This is probably why the government will not concede liability.

1,500 are still alive today. At the time, politicians in power covered up the truth about these health outcomes, kept the truth from fellow politicians who opposed the testing, and kept the service personnel under orders to remain silent. But the veterans came together to take this on. To this day, responsibility has not been acknowledged by the British government and huge sums of public money (£1.8m) have been spent defending their position that there was no valid evidence of causation. When the matter finally reached the Supreme Court in 2012, it was determined to be too late. It does not take much to work out who holds the moral high ground, and who the real victors are in this grim narrative.

CND was launched in February 1958 with a massive public meeting at the Central Hall in Westminster (a favoured venue for dissent, right opposite the Houses of Parliament). Its aim was to campaign against the very fallout experienced above, to promote disarmament at multilateral and unilateral levels, and at the least to prevent the proliferation of nuclear weapons (a goal that would eventually be achieved in the 1968 non-proliferation treaty. The Aldermaston marches, from London to the Atomic Weapons Research Establishment in Aldermaston, Berkshire, were flagship protests which risked arrest and political hostility but garnered a shift in public attitudes. They were augmented by more direct action fostered by the Committee of 100, led by the philosopher Bertrand Russell. A 4,000-strong mass sit-down took place outside the Ministry of Defence in Whitehall in 1961, and later that year over 1,000 were arrested in Trafalgar Square, including the 90-year-old Bertrand himself.

The momentum continued with the historic and influential mass demonstrations of opposition to the Vietnam War and especially, later, the deployment of cruise missiles. The Greenham Common women's peace camp and the act of women encircling RAF Greenham Common, where US Air Force cruise missiles were stationed, left an indelible imprint on the public conscience. This has re-emerged in the context of the war being waged presently by Russia in Ukraine, the threat of nuclear war and the deployment from the UK of depleted uranium, which has radioactive properties.

Michael Seifert – activist, solicitor and a dear friend from my school days – persuaded me about the importance of public protest in 1960 and I joined the annual Easter CND march that year. By 15 February 2003 and the anti-Iraq war demonstration, I was there with 1.5 million others, although I failed to recognise George Clooney standing 2 feet away at the start (which I know makes me sound like a somewhat elderly member of the judiciary!).

★

A third movement that stemmed from the same period – and is of equal force to the two discussed above – has an ongoing special significance to contemporary events: the Black Lives Matter movement.

After my mother's searing brush with the law in Whetstone, my life had continued its course in a very white suburb of North London and at very white schools in Woodside Park and Highgate, followed in 1960 by a predominantly white university (Keele in North Staffordshire). Matters did not improve by choosing a career at the Bar in 1967. Any encounters with the Windrush generation, or any of those arriving in Britain between 1948 and 1971, passed me by entirely. This was not a promising start for my appreciation of diversity and equality.

Fortunately, change was at hand with the help of certain individuals who were kind enough and perceptive enough to realise I was at sea – out of touch, in another world, a parallel universe. They brought me up shortly and firmly with what was happening in the real world, right under my nose, without me realising. I had met these people because I was lucky enough to be briefed by one of the finest and most committed solicitors in the country – Gareth Peirce – who was also involved in rectifying the miscarriages of justice discussed in the previous chapter. Much of what was occurring on the streets ended up being fought in the courts.

'No Irish, No blacks, No dogs' was a common notice outside boarding houses in London and Birmingham during the late 1950s and early 1960s. The arrivals, predominantly from Commonwealth Caribbean countries, had been invited to come to the United Kingdom after WW2 to help address post-war labour shortages, but they found themselves bereft with no homes and no ready palatable work. Hostility, prejudice and bigotry pervaded daily life, buttressed by an antagonistic police force. Increasingly, the resignation and acceptance of the older generation's approach – that's how it is – meant discrimination had become second nature in society. The dominant culture was one of abuse and exploitation.

My eyes, which had hitherto been looking in the wrong direction, were opened by what I heard and what I saw. The individuals who gently prodded me were Darcus Howe, Frank Crichlow and John La Rose, all of whom I would come to count as friends as time went on, but all of whom have sadly died over the last decade or so.

The outstanding and vivid memory I nurture to this day is the careful and caring way they ushered me through their lives and their experiences. On one occasion in the 1970s, they arrived together on a Sunday at my home unannounced and suggested I might like to hear what they had to say, given my involvement in cases emanating from the Black community. Even though I had met them individually before, I had no idea what was coming.

As I listened to them, they moved me just as they moved many others. I was shocked and remain shocked. It was the daily hostility and open comment; the regular discrimination; the body language; the physical assaults. It was often easier for them to deal with the spoken than the unspoken, the insidious. There had to be change, and for this to happen there had to be understanding and a strong drive for fairness. Respect was the key. I needed to grasp all this to represent the feelings, the conditions and the impediments of a community I was living among. It was as if I had been living in a parallel universe, within touching distance.

John La Rose and his wife Irma ran a bookshop – New Beacon Books in Stroud Green, North London – round the corner from my home at that time. John was an eminent writer and activist.

Akin to an elder statesman in his general demeanour, he was softly spoken with words kindly delivered and carefully crafted. John had been compared on more than one occasion to Marcus Garvey and CLR James. The bookshop itself was a haven and a repository of knowledge and his was the first specialist Caribbean publishing company in Britain.

Darcus Howe, like John, was from Trinidad and was a giant of a character, both mentally and physically. His presence and his intellect were felt wherever he went. A broadcaster known for his tireless campaigning, he inspired hope and possibility and was described as one of the great polemicists of his time. He was a powerful and incisive speaker who left you in no doubt about the need for action.

Frank Crichlow was a community worker and civil rights campaigner in Notting Hill, and was often seen as the godfather of Black radicalism. His beliefs entailed a practical resolution to the obvious inequalities. He was instrumental in the development of the Notting Hill Carnival and in the late 1960s opened a restaurant called the Mangrove, which doubled as an informal community centre and home to the Mangrove Community Association, set up to help drug addicts, alcoholics and ex-offenders. This made him an obvious target for the authorities and the police, who deliberately contrived false accusations about his activities. Local policeman PC Pulley, the renowned bane of the Black community in Notting Hill, referred to the Mangrove as a 'den of iniquity'.

Darcus Howe, Frank Crichlow and John La Rose were very much part of the movement that was gathering. They were all part of the community, and on the front line to such an extent that two of them were defendants in watershed trials. They provided confidence for those who were diffident and articulation for those who knew what to say but not how to say it.

I had met both Darcus and Frank in the lead-up to the first of the groundbreaking trials – the Mangrove Nine, in 1971. I had been instructed on behalf of one of the Nine, at what was then known as the 'committal stage' before trial. In the end, I was unable to be present at the trial because of other commitments, but my friend and colleague, the late Ian Macdonald, was involved throughout.

The trial had arisen because the Mangrove restaurant and community hub Frank had opened in 1968 on All Saints Road in Notting Hill was viewed as a hotbed of illegality. This was the year Enoch Powell MP addressed Conservatives in Birmingham with a notorious speech, tagged thereafter as the Rivers of Blood speech. Powell raised the spectre of Wolverhampton and the rest of the United Kingdom being swamped by immigrants. He claimed one local school had only one white child. Powell's ideology meant that the flood had to be dammed, or even reversed, by means of repatriation to circumvent insurrection on the streets. There is an echo of this in the latest Tory thoughts on immigration. Suella Braverman – barrister, ex-Attorney General and current Home Secretary – prefers 'invasion' to 'flood', and 'deportation' to 'repatriation', even when the destination of Rwanda is unsafe and unlawful.

The Mangrove was raided numerous times in 1969 and 1970 – approximately twelve times without any evidence of armed revolution, drugs or anything untoward being found. The point had been reached, as it had been in other arenas, where the ordinary citizen was not going to accept victim status and roll over any more. This was the red line in the sand.

On 9 August 1970, a peaceful protest march of roughly 150 Black citizens was organised to Notting Hill police station. They were met by a phalanx of 588 constables, 84 sergeants, 29 inspectors and 4 chief inspectors – not exactly a conciliatory nor understanding approach to race relations. All the usual preconceptions contaminated the way the Black community was perceived and treated.

Violent altercations ensued and nine people were charged with a variety of offences, the most serious of which was incitement to riot. The Nine were Frank Crichlow, Darcus Howe, Barbara Beese, Rhodan Gordon, Rupert Boyce, Altheia Jones LeCointe, Rothwell Kentish, Godfrey Millett and Anthony Innis.

The committing magistrate initially dismissed the case, but the Director of Public Prosecutions reinstated it and the Nine found themselves at the Old Bailey in front of a well-known, stern and authoritarian judge, Edward Clarke QC. The way the defence was conducted undoubtedly broke new ground and caused ripples of concern throughout the establishment. One main feature of the trial was that two of the defendants, Darcus and Altheia, represented themselves – a bold and extremely rare occurrence then, save of course for the historic exploits of my dear old Mum.

This enabled them to make legal submissions, to cross-examine witnesses (especially police officers), to address the jury directly by an opening or a closing speech on their own behalf, in addition to giving evidence themselves. This highly effective strategy has been captured by Steve McQueen's poignant film *Mangrove* (2020).

The fifty-five-day trial also ensured that race and discrimination were centre stage from the start, when there were extensive submissions applying for a Black-only jury panel. In 1971, this was a novel argument which had not been canvassed before. It was rejected, but by using the right of each defendant to peremptory challenge without cause*, it was possible to at least achieve some Black representation on the jury.

All Nine were acquitted of the main counts relating to riot and, quite unexpectedly, the judge acknowledged that

---

* Peremptory challenge without cause allowed defendants to challenge the inclusion of certain individuals on a jury without needing to give a reason. At the time of the Mangrove trial, up to seven jury members could be dismissed. This was reduced to three in 1977, and abolished altogether in 1988.

the trial had 'regrettably shown evidence of racial hatred'. The warning flare had been fired. The push for change could not be stopped.

In the years that followed, Frank was pursued and harassed endlessly. Because nothing was ever found, the police either fabricated what they claimed to see or took drugs onto the premises to plant on Frank himself. I represented him more than once at Knightsbridge Crown Court. Each time he was acquitted. Each time his resolve remained to carry on regardless, for the benefit of a strong hinterland of need and support. A decade later, the force for change had grown enormously.

In the early hours of Sunday 18 January 1981, a terrible fire broke out during a party at a house in New Cross, Southeast London, claiming the lives of 13 young Black people. At the time, there was a strong suspicion that the fire might have been started deliberately.

The New Cross Action Committee was established promptly, chaired by John La Rose. Its objective was to provide support and advice to the many parents and friends and to act as a crucible for the distinct feelings of anger throughout the Black community, not only over the fire but many other issues that had been troubling over the past decade.

A National Black People's Day of Action was organised for 2 March, which saw an estimated 20,000 people marching for several hours through the streets of London. One of the striking slogans was '13 dead, nothing said'*. It was unquestionably the largest mass movement for social justice up to that time and is featured in another Steve McQueen film, *Uprising* (2001). Its impact cannot be underestimated.

The relatives of those who died in the fire have maintained an active campaign over the years, partly because no one believes the whole story has yet been uncovered. There have been two inquests into the fire, the first in 1981 at which I represented some of the families, and the second in 2004. Both of the inquests returned open verdicts.

This is not the place to re-examine the evidence about the seat of the fire and its origin. My point is different. It is that the tenacity of the families and their friends has kept the spirit of truth alive, and the original campaign jolted the British public a little further towards the realisation of a racially just society.

★

---

* This slogan was commemorated by Benjamin Zephaniah in his poem *13 Dead*. Zephaniah spent a year in my chambers, Tooks, as the poet in residence.

This jolt was accelerated by events in Brixton, South London, three months later. At the beginning of April 1981, the Metropolitan Police began another of their heavy-handed operations – suitably named Swamp 81 – on the pretext of combating street crime. They used the primeval powers contained in Section 4 of the 1824 Vagrancy Act, which endowed police officers with a discretionary power to arrest anyone they suspected of loitering with intent to commit an arrestable offence. These powers were known as the 'sus' laws and incorporated stop and search. The power was used disproportionately against the Black population, who fitted police preconceptions about the usual suspect*.

Unsurprisingly, as in Notting Hill, this police strategy inevitably provoked an angry response, and an uprising ensued, lasting for two days between 10 and 12 April. The Home Secretary commissioned an inquiry into the disturbances, headed by Lord Scarman.

I attended some of the inquiry hearings as an observer and felt that it was unlikely to shake the foundations of prejudice. Lord Scarman was urbane and academic, with a sharp intellect and attentive manner, and probably had the most distinctively memorable features of any judge – he

---

* The Runnymede Trust had compiled a report in 1978, which identified this problem.

was described by Stephen Sedley as 'an ascetic's face lit by charm'. He was chair of the Law Commission for eight years and had also chaired the Red Lion Square Inquiry, involving a young Warwick University student, Kevin Gately, who had died from head injuries on an anti-fascist demonstration. I had represented his family at the inquest.

Part of the problem was Lord Scarman's refusal to examine complaints of police misconduct. He suggested instead they should be channelled through the police complaints system, which was not trusted. This seriously undermined local public confidence in the inquiry.

The truth was that racism was endemic and needed to be tackled head on, just as it does now. Lord Scarman certainly identified aspects of social and economic disadvantage as part of inner city decline and counselled urgent action to prevent it becoming an 'ineradicable disease threatening the very survival of our society'. He was also highly critical of the indiscriminate use of stop and search powers.

Perhaps he felt constrained by the tenor or the pressures of established thinking, but it is bewildering that he was unable to discern the institutional nature of the racism, which his report found did not exist. This conclusion would not be upheld over a decade later by another member of the senior judiciary in the Lawrence Inquiry report, chaired by Sir William Macpherson.

The die had, however, been cast. There were strong vibrations at ground level which would continue throughout that decade and beyond. Growing resilience and resurgence were instilling confidence. This was embodied, remarkably, in a singular fashion by the school at the centre of Enoch Powell's toxic rhetoric in his Rivers of Blood speech – West Park Primary. The school confronted and harnessed its notoriety through its pride in diversity and integration. In 2017, it turned the tide with a history project entitled West Park Welcomes the World.

Chapter 4
A New Horizon

In my job, when you are first approached to consider taking on a case, its true import or significance may not be apparent. That it may transform the legal, political and social landscape is certainly not a thought that springs to mind. It is rarely ever clear where a case might lead and it is imperative to keep an open mind about ultimate outcomes.

The murder of Stephen Lawrence, however, had a strangely different feel to it. It's now been thirty years since Stephen's death – on 22 April 1993 – and I recently had the honour of being able to attend the memorial.

The facts of his murder have been traversed many times in the public domain, in plays, books, films and documentaries. It's not my intention, therefore, to rehearse all the evidence surrounding this brutal racist attack by a group of well-known white thugs in Eltham, Southeast London. Stephen, a Black British man aged just 18 years old, was murdered in an unprovoked attack at a bus stop in Well Hall Road while returning home with his friend Duwayne Brooks. The assailants had announced their attack with the words 'What, what n . . .'.

Instead, I would like to focus on the quite remarkable resilience shown by Stephen's bereft parents, Neville and Doreen, and their determination from the moment of the murder to achieve accountability and radical change.

What was different on this occasion was the nature of the task I was being asked to undertake. Imran Khan – now KC but then an assiduous, newly qualified and truly dedicated radical solicitor – wanted me to represent the Lawrence family at the opening of an inquest in 1993 and also provide advice in relation to their relationship with the police investigation. I would not normally perform this latter role, but I recognised it could be vitally important, not just for the inquest in the long term but also for getting answers about what had happened in the short term. But at that point, the case itself, sadly, seemed like too many others I had handled over the previous 25 years.

It was not long before I realised this case had a different dimension, a burning and unrelenting quest for answers that were not patronising or dismissive. At its heart was an issue of respect. Respect for the needs of those most closely affected, and respect for the core values of objective police investigation. There would be no closure for the family, friends and the wider Black community until this was acknowledged and processes had been rectified. Stephen's parents were two straightforward, straight-thinking, ordinary members of the public suddenly catapulted into an alien environment in which they were being expected to act as passive and grateful recipients of whatever platitudinous offerings were being made available. What had to be done became abundantly clear to both Imran and me. But it would take persistence, patience and considerable courage. Standing shoulder to shoulder would be crucial.

Thirty years on, a week after the 2023 memorial, the same undeterred determination shone through the softly spoken reflections of Stephen's father, Neville. I wanted to catch up on how he was feeling. He was keen to reiterate key messages for the next generation, those he had impressed upon me when we first met. 'Never take no for an answer', 'Never give up' and 'Never do nothing'. That, of course, is what those in power want, nay even expect. That way they bank on people's troublesome questions dissipating into the mists of time.

In the days that followed the murder, the Lawrence home was flooded with family, friends and well-wishers. Two regular visitors were police liaison officers John Bevan and Linda Holden, whose task was to liaise with the incident room. Of interest given later events, they asked more questions than they answered and the Lawrences felt they were kept 'in the dark'. This affords a chapter title in Doreen's reflective book on this story, *And Still I Rise* (2007). What was really going on and what undercover infiltration was being carried out is now the subject of the Undercover Policing Inquiry, in which Doreen, Neville and myself have core participant status. For that reason, I cannot comment further at present.

There were obvious questions to be pressed, especially relating to what is termed the 'golden first hours' of an investigation into a recently committed crime. Primarily, there is often information about potential perpetrators and there was no wall of silence here, as was asserted by police sources. In fact, some of the community had provided names to Doreen and Neville. That usually puts prompt surveillance on high priority – eyewitnesses need to be traced before memories fade, and the preservation of the scene and the victim's clothing are other priorities.

As it turned out, the police were grossly negligent in all these areas. Within hours they had names and information, particularly from an informant anonymised as 'James Grant', but they did not pursue this information expeditiously. Grant attended Plumstead police station on Friday 23 April, the day after the murder, at 7.45pm. The subsequent Macpherson Inquiry recognised this information as the most important of all. The full account is set out in my memoirs from a police record. Message

40 contains the names of the two Acourt brothers – Jamie and Neil – and that of David Norris. Detailed descriptions together with an address were provided. Other information given to police gave even more detail, confirmed these names and added two more, those of Gary Dobson and Luke Knight.

No serious attempt was made to follow up this timely material, and dilatory outside inquiries were led by one of Grant's handlers, DS John Davidson (whose nickname within the force was 'OJ', Objectionable Jock – a name he certainly lived up to in the witness box during the inquiry). The information and James Grant himself were all marginalised. The only action took place four days later when a lone police photographer was posted outside the Acourt address and was able to record first Neil, and then Jamie, leaving the premises with black plastic bin bags! They were not followed to see what happened and what was in the bags, and they were not arrested until 7 May. These arrests should have seen the family forewarned confidentially, but Doreen first learned about the arrests on the news.

There was distinct soft pedalling from the police. The big question is why? The stark and unequivocal finding of the Macpherson Inquiry provides part of the answer: 'institutional racism'. The automatic unspoken reaction by police – implicitly understood from the off, although denied later – was that this case had nothing to do with race. They supposed it was some kind of drug deal between gangs that had gone wrong. This was fuelled by the knowledge that some of the names connected to the suspects had strong links with heavy mainstream crime (for example, Norris was an extremely familiar name).

While the Macpherson Inquiry found institutional racism, it was not prepared to find corruption. On behalf of the family, we had strongly argued this contention, given the circumstantial evidence. The problem with this proposition was it required a higher standard or threshold of proof as a criminal allegation – namely we had to satisfy the inquiry panel beyond reasonable doubt. We thought we had, but the panel disagreed. We await with interest what is uncovered by the Undercover Policing Inquiry in relation to the Stephen Lawrence case.

On the truth trail, Mr and Mrs Lawrence felt thoroughly isolated from the whole investigative process and thwarted at every twist and turn. That is, until 6 May and a fortuitous and unexpected intervention from the most eminent Black politician in the world, Nelson Mandela.

This had been facilitated by a well-connected journalist, Marc Wadsworth. Neville and Doreen met Nelson at a hotel in London. They had one thing upmost in common with him: insisting that there can be no justice without truth. In her book, Doreen recalled his observations to her: 'What horrified him was that he was used to racists killing with impunity in South Africa, but that it was not something he expected to see happening here in the UK.'

The contrast between the time, interest and spoken support from South Africa and the silence of domestic authorities, in particular Michael Howard, the Home Secretary, was telling. At a widely reported press conference, Nelson Mandela repeated his sentiments by saying, 'The Lawrence tragedy is our tragedy. I am deeply touched by the brutality of the murder – brutality that we are all used to in South Africa where black lives are cheap.'

The following day, the arrests were eventually made by police. This is officially a coincidence.

No Prosecution by the State

Doreen attended meetings with the police, accompanied by Imran, but they made little progress and rarely was she addressed directly. It was as if she did not exist. When she took the trouble to commit the information she had received about the perpetrators to paper for the assistance of the police, she watched during the first meeting as Detective Chief Superintendent Bill Ilsley folded that piece of paper into increasingly small squares. Having said nothing in the meeting, she remarked on the way out that no doubt the tiny square was destined for the bin. In the light of her searing comment, it wasn't, and when produced at later proceedings, the fold marks were all too evident and drawn to the attention of the jury by the coroner at the inquest.

Alongside this was the trauma of death which had to be absorbed. The release of Stephen's body was not straightforward, with potential criminal proceedings pending after the arrests. Ultimately, he was buried in Jamaica. There were two reasons. The first was Stephen's love of Jamaica, but the second reveals an ever-present and pervasive substratum of racism and hate on the streets, which we must all confront.

Neville and Doreen felt threatened themselves after the murder and were concerned that were Stephen to be buried in the UK, his grave would be desecrated. Their fears were unutterably justified. The plaque on the pavement in Well Hall Road, marking the spot where Stephen was fatally stabbed, has been seriously damaged on at least four or five occasions by a chisel, paint, flammable liquids and shards of glass, such that it has had to be replaced and a camera installed.

The murder and repercussions of this kind, to use Neville's words, 'have torn my family apart. I've lost not only my son but also my other children and grandchildren who live here while I live in Jamaica to be with Stephen.'

Although five suspects were arrested, only two were charged, primarily based on identification evidence, and those charges were dropped within months as the Crown Prosecution Service assessed there was insufficient evidence to provide a realistic prospect of conviction. Once again, there had been no forewarning for the family, who were still in Jamaica for Stephen's funeral. It was an emotional bombshell.

It took its toll, but public support became vociferous. Demonstrations, vigils, meetings, marches all played a necessary part in keeping the flame alight. There was hardly a private moment for the family, a moment to breathe, to adjust. Yet the most amazing transformation took place in front of me – neither Doreen nor Neville had been accustomed to speaking publicly to large numbers of people, let alone about such personal matters, but they stepped up to the challenge. It did not take long, but it did take an enormous leap of faith for each of them.

I was privileged to play a small part in this, having been through this experience over a much longer professional career. In the end, whatever it is you want to say, take a deep breath, take your time, wait for your brain and the audience to settle, keep it clear and simple, and remember that human powers of concentration fade after 20 minutes! Both Neville and Doreen soon captured hearts and minds.

Neville explained during our recent conversation that he had noticed how in America, when there was a civil rights issue, members of the clergy were often close by the family and would act as spokespersons. Martin Luther King was a Baptist minister. 'I did not have that support, but I found it with others – the Black section of the trade unions, they came to my house. I was invited to the TUC conference. I prepared some leaflets about the case to hand to delegates but I was persuaded it would be more effective to speak.'

This would be a daunting and nerve-wracking prospect for anyone. He was allotted a prime spot. A short wait ensued while he rose and then a longer pause before any words were spoken. There was a respectful if not anxious anticipation and a pin-dropping silence. Neville spoke from the heart in a measured and compelling tone. It was a natural masterpiece and the audience stood as one to applaud.

The Barker Review

To offset the calls for a public inquiry, it was decided there would be an internal review of the case under the command of Detective Chief Superintendent John Barker*. For a fleeting moment the Lawrences thought someone was

---

* The Barker Review in August 1993.

listening and that the sequence of one disappointment after another might be stemmed. That was a short-lived moment. By November this review, deeply flawed as it later turned out, had concluded:

> The investigation had been progressed satisfactorily and all lines of inquiry correctly pursued.

This was another setback, but also a spur. There comes a time when you are almost expecting more of the same, so you are already planning the next move because your resolve has hardened against the forces of darkness.

There was still the inquest to come, which we requested be adjourned while more investigation took place and to avoid prejudice to any remaining potential prosecutions. This was granted and, shortly after, the Commissioner of the Met, Paul Condon, finally agreed in the spring of 1994 to meet Mr and Mrs Lawrence. He instigated, reluctantly, a reinvestigation. A raft of new information came to light and we had a brainstorming meeting to consider a more assertive approach. Part of that reassessment was whether we should launch a private prosecution. This is a high-risk strategy. Very few private prosecutions are initiated because there is a funding issue, which had already impacted the inquest proceedings. It would necessarily depend on co-operation from the new team of police investigators who, for all we knew, might not be any better than the last lot. Ultimately, the Director of Public Prosecutions (DPP) retains a discretion to intervene, even if we got it off the ground, and then to discontinue either because it does not reach the evidential threshold or because it is not in the public interest.

Some of the new material had been obtained by secret audio and camera recordings in premises frequented by the suspects. The content was shocking and demonstrated a number of relevant important aspects: quite abhorrent racist language and attitudes (later described by the Macpherson report as 'gross and revolting'); an obsession with knives and how they might inflict wounds in a manner consistent with the wounds inflicted on Stephen; and a nonchalant glorification about the possibility they were under police surveillance. On one of the tapes*, Neil Acourt is heard to remark, 'I reckon that every n . . . should be chopped up, mate, and they should be left with nothing but fucking stumps.' Compelling though all this was, it would present complex arguments about admissibility in any court proceedings.

---

* A transcript of the tapes was produced and their veracity and integrity were never questioned. The recording device was contained in a floor-level electrical plug point in the living room of their abode.

The Private Prosecution

Despite all the pitfalls, the united consensus among the Lawrences' team was to forge ahead with a private prosecution and keep the inquest on the back burner. None of this was easy because every stage meant Doreen and Neville had to go through the whole picture of Stephen's demise again.

In a private prosecution, I appear for the prosecution on behalf of the family, not the state. Nevertheless, it has to be conducted in accordance with all the principles of a public prosecution, for example in relation to the prosecutorial code and disclosure. But unlike a public prosecution, the family is intimately involved at all stages.

There were three main pillars of evidence: identification by Stephen's friend Duwayne Brooks (the three witnesses at the bus stop were unable to do so); forensic science trace connections; and undercover recordings of severe racist intent and propensity.

We were acutely aware that all were vulnerable areas. Duwayne had suffered the trauma of the event, seeing his friend killed and having a near escape himself; the trace evidence in terms of fibres was not definitive; and the recordings were done after the murder and did not contain a direct admission. In addition, we were aware that there were serious attempts being made to undermine Duwayne's credibility – he was the subject of criminal charges arising from an anti-British National Party protest (which were dismissed in December 1994). Personally, I had always felt that his initial written statement, taken a few hours after the event, was incredibly impressive and lucid, especially regarding the clothing worn by the attackers, the individuals in the group and the circumstances. The problem came with later statements, where there were discrepancies.

A prosecution case was, however, assembled. The first hurdle was once again the committal stage in front of a magistrate. We needed the police to help with locating and arresting all five identified suspects. When everything was in place, the hearings began in the courts adjoining Belmarsh Prison in Woolwich, Southeast London, on Wednesday 23 August 1995, before Judge David Cooper.

Public interest was enormous, and the press benches were packed. We had to ensure spaces had been reserved for Neville and Doreen. For them, for the first time since the murder, they would be sitting in the same room as the familiar named suspects, a few feet from the dock, with the suspects' friends and relatives close by in the public gallery. A satisfying but nerve-wracking moment. The whole procedure is not just a formality because the magistrate has an onerous task of scrutiny to ensure the evidence is capable of being relied upon and constitutes a case to answer.

Besides the forbidding presence of the five defendants, Doreen and Neville had to endure hearing the distressing pathological detail, the aggressively obscene and offensive attitudes expressed on the covert surveillance, and Duwayne's account of the fatal assault. There were occasions when it was all too much. Overwhelming grief and anger tore through their hearts and at critical stages they both had to sit outside to recuperate.

The Committing Magistrate found in our favour in relation to three of the five suspects – Neil Acourt, Luke Knight and Gary Dobson. The next stop was the Old Bailey for trial by jury, unless the DPP intervened. He did not.

Doreen released a poignant and powerful statement, which she records in her book:

> It has been two years now since the Crown Prosecution dropped the charges against two men for the murder of our son, without even caring to consult or advise us of their decision. It was an act as hurtful and as painful in its effect as the news that Stephen had been killed. Since that time we have fought against tremendous obstacles to reach this stage. These obstacles have been overcome by our own private efforts, with the help of our family and many supporters who have joined us along the way, and at great financial risk . . . No family should ever experience

the last two years of our lives. This is the worst kind of fame. We have been brought into the public spotlight not by our own acts, but by the failure of others who were under a public duty to act. The decision of the court today stands as the first clear indictment of that failure.

At this juncture, we were not even halfway through the whole distressing story, not that anyone realised that at the time. I am relating it in detail here because while nobody should be under any illusion about what is entailed by a challenge to those in power, it should never be allowed to shroud the truth or deter the quest for justice. Conversely, no one in power should believe for one moment that they can succeed by simply engaging in a slow, wearing war of attrition, obstruction and denial. Ultimately, this tale of two citizens has a clear and singular message, one of enduring aspiration and achievement within the reach of every citizen.

The trial was set down before Mr Justice Curtis at the Old Bailey, in the famous, main oak-panelled courtroom – Number 1 – which has seen many historic trials unfold. It can be a daunting prospect for anyone, quite a different atmosphere from the Magistrates' Court. At the Bailey, robes and wigs abound; ceremony colours every move and every antiquated word, where lawyers on opposing sides refer to each other as 'learned friends'. Not exactly the parlance of daily conversation or altercation. Another alien world to be engaged by Mr and Mrs Lawrence.

As anticipated, the defence gave notice that there were preliminary matters of law they wished to raise. The main one related to the reliability of the identification evidence and its admissibility. The procedure for resolving this is a 'voir dire' (a preliminary trial within a trial) in the absence of the jury. Our position regarding the evidence that had survived the committal stage was that any points of criticism were matters of weight for the jury and did not invalidate the evidence altogether. After a week of argument and evidence on this issue, the judge disagreed and ruled out all of it. I had opened the case to the jury without referring to matters subject to legal challenge, so this left us with a huge dilemma.

Although we may not display emotion at moments like this, I was dismayed beyond belief. I asked the judge for time to consider our position. Imran, solicitor Caron Thatcher, Neville and Doreen, myself and my team – Steve Kamlish, Margo Boye-Anawoma and Martin Soorjoo – all retired to a private room. We all knew we were in a melting pot, on show to the world. It was probably one of the most unpalatable duties I have ever had to perform. A major hole had been shot through the centre of our case and, realistically, none of us could fill it with what remained. Rather than protract and defer the inevitable, it was agreed I should discontinue and offer no further evidence.

Doreen collapsed, exhausted and deflated. She left the Old Bailey in a wheelchair and was taken home by Neville and friends.

Each one of us felt empty, completely drained, particularly when I informed the judge of our decision, who then instructed the jury in time-honoured terms to return verdicts of 'not guilty' in relation to all three defendants.

A necessary period of retreat and reflection followed. Nights with no sleep. Days with scant food. Extreme distress. But the phoenix was rising as it had to. The deep-seated force for justice cannot be suppressed.

The Inquest

It is claimed that time is a great healer, but I feel it is more a great motivator. By February 1997, the wounds of injustice were as raw as ever. The infamous Five probably thought they could brazen their way out of the tightest corners. But no one quite bargained for how it would all roll out, let alone the trajectory which would eventually take us all into orbit!

It was yet another court appearance. Southwark Coroner's Court before a jury and the coroner, Sir Montague Levine – larger than life and Dickensian in appearance, with a glorious handlebar moustache. He took time to speak privately to Doreen and Neville before the inquest proceedings entered the final phase. In those days, that was not a common occurrence. He explained the process and offered very sincere condolences. It was to be his last inquest.

The object of an inquest is fourfold: to establish who the deceased was, when and where he died, and – fourthly and the crucial bit – how he died. The last is always the key question, particularly here because it related to the five suspects. While none of them had been convicted, the inquest had an overall function to deal with and dispel rumour, part of which centred on allegations against the men. During an inquest, no one is on trial and witnesses are protected by a rule against self-incrimination. On this basis, the Five were summoned to give evidence. Once more, the Lawrence family had to steel themselves for a close encounter.

Doreen went first. The force of passion and the clarity of critique hit every home in the country. If this could happen to her and Neville, it could happen to any Black family. Who would be next?

Sir Montague was both experienced and sensitive to the occasion; he knew the family needed this opportunity to bare their souls and chart the stormy waters. Doreen stood up and said, 'When my son was murdered, the police said my son was a criminal belonging to a gang.

My son was stereotyped by the police – he was Black then he must be a criminal – and they set about investigating him and us. My son's crime is that he was walking down the road looking for a bus that would take him home. Our crime is living in a country where the justice system supports racist murderers against innocent people . . . To the Black community: your lives are nothing. You do not have any rights to the law in this country'. There was more, much more.

Next came the Five – arrogant and unashamed. They performed as if it were a pantomime or some kind of Whitehall farce. Each invoked the privilege against self-incrimination and thought it would be super-sharp not to even acknowledge who they were, let alone where they were on the day. This is a plain abuse of the privilege and the coroner asked their legal representatives to proffer advice. Nothing changed. Little did they realise, this was to be another turning point.

Their insolence spoke volumes and led the jury to return a momentous verdict:

> Stephen Lawrence was unlawfully killed in a completely
> unprovoked racist attack by five white youths.

This jury was able to fulfil what the jury at the Old Bailey was not given the opportunity to do. It's as near as a Coroner's Court can come, without breaching the prohibition on determining criminal liability. By adding the words 'five white youths' the die was cast for the next decade.

The Macpherson Inquiry –
The Force is with You

The day after the verdict, the *Daily Mail* blazoned a simple one-word headline above photographs of the Five: 'MURDERERS'. It accused them of killing Stephen and invited them to sue if this was wrong.

However this tactic is viewed, it certainly stirred consciences and contributed to the pressure for action. I phrase this guardedly because, ironically, Doreen is herself (along with others including Elton John and Hugh Grant) suing the publisher of the *Daily Mail*, alleging that they hired private investigators to hack her phone and obtain information on Stephen. According to a *Guardian* report on 27 March 2023, 'She believes she failed her murdered son by trusting the *Daily Mail* in the 1990s when the news outlet only campaigned for justice in a cynical bid to sell more newspapers.'

Other factors ratcheted up the pressure for action. One was the volte-face of the police during the inquest in maintaining that there had been nothing wrong with the original investigation. Another was a review that had been ordered into issues surrounding the case to be carried out by the Kent Constabulary; and a third was that there was a change of government, with Jack Straw becoming Home Secretary.

On 24 June 1997, I accompanied the family and Imran to meet him. Doreen was clear she would not be happy with a report filled with platitudes and generalities about community and race relations. She was worried that it might be another Scarman report* which would languish on some back shelf in Whitehall or, worse, another review and not an inquiry at all.

Meanwhile, the Kent police review was published in December and found 'significant weaknesses, omissions and lost opportunities in the conduct of the case'.

A Judicial Public Inquiry was announced 'to examine the circumstances surrounding Stephen's death' and 'to identify the lessons to be learned for the investigation and the prosecution of racially motivated crimes'. It opened in March 1998 in a large conference room above the incongruously pink shopping mall in the centre of Elephant and Castle in London. The chair was a retired High Court judge, Sir William Macpherson of Cluny, assisted by a panel comprising Bishop John Sentamu

---

* A report commissioned by the government following the Brixton Riots in 1981 (see Chapter 3, page 51).

(who went on to become Archbishop of York); Tom Cook (former Deputy Chief Constable of West Yorkshire Police) and Dr Richard Stone (GP and Chair of the Jewish Council for Racial Equality).

This was indeed a formidable panel. It represented a notable milestone, which reinvigorated flagging spirits. It lifted the possibility of public accountability and change firmly onto the national agenda. There was a slight hiccup, however, as unease was expressed in some quarters that Sir William, with his austere family and military background, and the severity of some of his judgements, might not be an appropriate choice.

There was consternation within the family, so I advised we request a short breathing space for reflection. Mounting a challenge to a judge on these grounds is uncommon and necessarily delicate, especially if it is unsuccessful! Normally it takes the form of an application to the judge to recuse himself; for example, if he has a vested interest in the outcome or has expressed strong views about the issues in hand.

It was relatively well known that I had managed to get the Lord Chief Justice, Lord Lane, to stand down in a case concerning the 1984 miners' strike. However, this was not comparable. I felt we should tread carefully. Rather than making a fuss in public, which would definitely screw the pitch, it might be better to consult with the Home Secretary. This could not be done with a flick of the finger. Was he available, would he feel able to see us? Secondly, I would, as a matter of courtesy, have to inform Sir William in private why we needed a short adjournment. He might be naturally perturbed or, worse, he might object and just tell us to get on with it, as would be his prerogative. But in fact he was none of these things. As I rapidly discovered, Sir William was plain-speaking, decisive and circumspect.

Both he and the Home Secretary were only too conscious of the public relations disaster if this was not sorted. Jack Straw explained to Doreen that the bottom line was finding a judge of the right seniority, who was not only free to take on such an onerous task, but was also willing to do it. At short notice, this could not be done and would lead to unacceptable delay. In any event, he continued, he was not sitting as a lone arbiter – the other panellists would provide informed balance and diversity. Doreen's fears were assuaged.

The hearings lasted for nine months, commencing on 24 March 1998. It did not take long to discern that the officer qualities in Sir William were finding it difficult to countenance the incompetence of the senior ranking police. An unusually large number of high-ranking officers turned up at the scene and contributed next to nothing.

The five thugs were summoned for a second performance of their tiresome act. They did not disappoint, and were described by Sir William as 'arrogant and dismissive, evasive and vague'.

They arrived together and left together. They were met by a large hostile crowd outside and rose to the occasion by displaying their customary aggression. The disruptive scenes outside the inquiry were broadcast across all news channels.

There were two parts to the hearings. The first dealt with the circumstances of the murder and its investigation, and the second listened to community groups and others about the lessons which could be learned.

The report produced by Sir William and his co-panellists was unquestionably a masterpiece. It would come to be regarded by many as a landmark in judicial history in the way it created a new framework and tackled recalcitrant institutions, and a landmark in the history of race relations. The main finding of 'institutional racism' sent shock waves through the establishment. They could deal with rooting out the odd 'bad apple in the barrel' but not the possibility of the whole barrel being bad. The report contained a series of seventy carefully crafted recommendations for better investigation and prosecution of race crime. They covered a broad range of topics and touched on areas well beyond policing itself. It could be said that it was a national alert for many institutions and for endemic racism generally.

We were all elated – a rare zenith. Our collective effort had taken us from a nadir of failure to a result we could not have predicted. Sir William and the whole panel need to be eternally credited for providing the loudest wake-up call since WW2.

Besides definitions of racism, the report covered accountability, training and education in diversity awareness, complaints, and the treatment of victims and witnesses. Legislation ensued, particularly amendments to the Race Relations Act, to cover the police service as a whole and all central government bodies.

In February 1999, just before the report was published, Jack Straw encapsulated the essence of this initiative (and all the other movements described in this book) by declaring, 'I want this report to act as a catalyst for fundamental and irreversible change across the whole of society.'

An astonishing achievement had been brought about by the sheer determination of the basic human force for justice and fairness in the face of adversity. It did not end there, but it indelibly marked out the territory and the boundaries.

Power Vacuum – A Blind Eye

The report was not received well by the police, some of whom regarded it as a betrayal. Initially there was considerable resistance and, regrettably, that still rumbles on today, preventing a developed and coherent anti-racist regime. It became manifest when, two decades later, in 2020, Cressida Dick (the first woman Commissioner of the Met) distanced herself from the conclusion of institutional racism and claimed it was not helpful. This was in the context of the quite shocking revelations about police attitudes on her watch. On 1 February 2022, the Independent Office for Police Conduct (IOPC) reported that 'disgraceful' discrimination, misogyny, homophobia, racism, bullying and harassment had occurred between 2016 and 2018 in a police station – Charing Cross – just down the road from New Scotland Yard. Her successor, Sir Mark Rowley, regurgitated the same corporate line and was equally unreceptive when confronted by Baroness Stacey's review, published in 2023, which not only reaffirmed the Macpherson finding, but also that of the IOPC – misogyny, deep-seated homophobia, bullying and sexism in the force.

Finally, last – and certainly least – is the Home Secretary, Suella Braverman, who came up with exactly the same assessment, noting that institutional racism is 'not a helpful term to use – ambiguous, contested, and politically charged'. This is somewhat rich from someone who revels in her own choice of inflammatory language.

It was precisely this institutional intransigence by those in power that led to Neville and Doreen's catastrophic collapse of faith in both the Met and the Home Office. It demonstrates that despite all their years of pain and anguish, and the intensive work of inquiry by responsible bodies, progress is still being thwarted. They feel strongly that it is an insult to the memory of Stephen and displays a shocking lack of respect.

The breakdown is so bad that Neville has said he 'would not ask a Met officer the way or the time of day as I did when I first arrived. And I would not want the Met to investigate Stephen's case any more in future.' He already has another police force in mind, which he feels is capable of being trusted to carry the investigation forward.

This high-level 'institutional denial' goes to show how ingrained the problem remains. It can hardly be countered if it is not admitted. This stance at the highest echelons can afford collusive permission – a culture in which a blind eye is cast.

The impediment stems from an instinctive rejection of what is perceived as a general tarnish of all police officers, allied to an inability or unwillingness to understand the notion of institutional racism. It is not a criticism of every police officer. It is the perpetuation of discrimination based on race inherent in the policies, practices, procedures and structure of the policing system – an in-built systemic prejudice.

According to the report, institutional racism 'can be seen or detected in processes, attitudes and behaviour which amount to discrimination through unwitting prejudice, ignorance, thoughtlessness, and racist stereotyping, which disadvantage minority ethnic people'. It can be conscious and deliberate, but mostly it is a conditioned cultural response. The report described 'the collective failure of an organisation to provide an appropriate and professional service to people because of their colour, culture or ethnic origin'.

The Aftermath – Who Guards the Guardians?

For all the reasons above, Sir William was anxious that the work he and his panel had devoted to the recommendations was not consigned to a filing cabinet. Time and again he insisted on extracting undertakings from those in authority that they would commit to implementation within a reasonable time. If the authorities had been left to their own devices, this report would have been emasculated and any action delayed or fudged. Ordinary people can do extraordinary things, but at the same time it needs extraordinary people to step up and do some ordinary things.

To facilitate such a possibility and to prevent political rigor mortis setting in, the Lawrence family inaugurated a process which had never been done before and should be a necessary consequence of all inquiries where there are proposals for the betterment of the public. Every year, starting in 2009, Doreen hired the Methodist Central Hall in Westminster, right opposite the Houses of Parliament, to hold the people in power to account. In other words, the key authorities were 'invited' to come along and explain how far they had got with implementing the seventy recommendations. This was not especially welcomed by Members of Parliament who had eagerly turned their minds to devolution and other matters of state.

The core injustice was that no one – no politician, no police officer, let alone any of the Five – had been brought to book. That being the case, it was necessary to find out if anything was going to be done about it and whether changes were going to be put into effect. The oxygen of publicity at the hands of a citizen who was riding high in popular sympathy was a remarkable stimulant. None of the relevant personages could afford not to be seen to attend. It was fast becoming an electoral issue.

Subsequent legislation – the Inquiries Act 2005 – has provided for the chair of an inquiry to be able to question, prior to the publication of its report, an incumbent government or any other authority that might be impacted by its recommendations, about the extent to which it intends to carry out the changes recommended. And if not, why not.

Truth Never Dies

So never give up. Neville and Doreen never did. At the end of Doreen's book – written before a further investigation, a prosecution and convictions, before a further corruption review and before a public inquiry (still ongoing) into undercover policing was announced – she honestly reflected that, 'Many a time I have felt like giving up. There were days, weeks or months when I felt I'd had enough, that I was bashing my head against a brick wall, that no one was listening or taking any notice. It was like going into combat every time I opened my front door, and no one gives an inch.'

That is exactly what 'they' want you to feel, and this no doubt resonates with every other campaign or movement for justice. For generations 'they' have banked on the fact that the ordinary person does not have the time, the energy, the resources or the patience to keep going and will just fade away. But commensurate with the recent decline and bankruptcy in our thinly democratic state, times have changed dramatically. The bare bones of indifference and autocratic authority have been exposed. In response, the citizen has stepped up more often and more strongly to provide a persistent challenging presence. Governments and Met Commissioners may come and go, but no matter what or who tries to sweep the shortcomings under the carpet, the continuing pressure of conspicuous injustice remains to remind each new person in power that the job is far from finished.

This is not how it used to be when I started in practice at the Bar in 1967. It is the emergence of this collective resilience that fuelled the crucial demands which, since the Macpherson report, produced two sets of important incremental results.

Firstly, another review of the whole case – this time, meticulous and painstaking. Led by DCI Clive Driscoll, the re-investigative team liaised closely with the Lawrence family. Critically, they procured the services of Dr Angela Gallop, a forensic scientist with whom I had worked over many years (including on the Cardiff Five case). Her byline was 'to infinity and beyond' and her methodology was impeccable. She had been involved on the original investigation.

Cold case reviews need to start afresh, from the very beginning. A return to the scene and a reconstruction often stimulates lateral thinking and gives rise to avenues of enquiry that have been under-explored. In the meantime, the technology of scene examination, trace collection and storage, and laboratory testing had progressed significantly.

All these factors had a bearing on where to look and what might be found, given the nature of the attack and the location. Dr Gallop's team discovered fibres, some of which we had at the time of the private prosecution. But this time two fibres compatible with Stephen's clothing were found embedded in a microscopic blood particle (deposited when wet), which matched the DNA of one of the five suspects, Dobson. This was found in the exhibit bag containing his jacket. Another speck was discovered in the collar region of the jacket. Detection and analysis of microscopic quantities had become more discerning. This was the killer in more senses than one. Fibres and a hair from Stephen also linked Norris.

Dobson and Norris both stood trial at the Old Bailey in 2011–12. They were convicted and sentenced at the end of a six-week trial. In the words of the trial judge, Mr Justice Treacy, 'this murder scarred the conscience of the nation'. For Doreen and Neville, it gave a modicum of closure. For me, personally, it was a taxing moment because I was a prosecution witness along with Dr Angela Gallop, dealing with the integrity and continuity of exhibits. You get a very different feeling in the witness box, rather than on the counsel's benches in the well of the court to which I was accustomed. I was somewhat uneasy at the prospect of having to answer questions rather than ask them, especially from counsel I knew!

The second positive development emerged from meetings we had with Theresa May when she was Home Secretary. Along with Jack Straw, she was one of the more accessible and involved Home Secretaries I have met over the years. Doreen and Neville had maintained a view that there had been a corrupt relationship between the police and the suspects. Although we could not satisfy Macpherson to the criminal standard of proof, we felt there was enough circumstantial material to at least merit further investigation. We provided our detailed inquiry submissions on this to the Home Secretary.

At the same time, there was another concern which had been 'bugging' the Lawrence household from the beginning – as it turns out, perhaps literally! They felt strongly that they had been under investigation and surveillance themselves, and that police had infiltrated and invaded their privacy.

Their suspicions on this front were heightened by the revelations in 2013 from Peter Francis, an ex-police officer and whistleblower who exposed the activities of the Special Demonstration Squad (SDS). The core allegation was that officers had been tasked to gather information on the Lawrence family to smear them and the campaign for justice.

Mark Ellison KC, who led the prosecution against Dobson and Norris, was tasked by the Home Secretary to carry out a review. His report shocked Theresa May, who described its findings as 'profoundly troubling and of grave concern' and consequently announced in 2015 that there would be a public inquiry into undercover policing. As mentioned earlier, both the Lawrences and I have been accorded the status of Core Participants and, as the inquiry is still current, I can say no more until its findings are published.

Among the issues raised by the Ellison review were failures to disclose material to be used in criminal proceedings, deception of the courts, failure to disclose allegations of corruption concerning DS Davidson to Macpherson and concerns about the deployment of undercover officers in the Stephen Lawrence family.

A Sixth Suspect –
the BBC Investigation

The true horror of this part of the story has only just become public – in June 2023 – following a BBC investigation, which revealed for the first time the name of a sixth suspect. Duwayne Brooks had always maintained the possibility of six assailants and had provided an important description of the sixth man to police – longish blonde hair, spiky or frizzy – which distinguished him from the other five suspects, all of whom had dark hair. Two other witnesses (Mr Westbrook and Mr Shepherd) gave similar descriptions to police.

This description fits a man called Matthew White, who died in 2021. The police knew this and White's name from the off. The information from 'James Grant' was incredibly precise and authoritative about who was responsible for the attack, such that he was either present himself or had been told by someone who was. According to Grant he had informed his handler, 'OJ' Davidson, that his source was someone who was present, namely Matthew White. Conveniently, the 'mishandler' had no satisfactory records of his dealings with Grant and had not registered him as an informant.

White's appearance was known to police – they even took a photograph of him outside the Acourt house a week or so after the murder, closely resembling the description of the sixth man they had been given. On the back of all this information, at the very least he should have been arrested – two weeks late though it was – with the other five suspects on 7 May 1993. Then he should have been placed on an identification parade for the three relevant witnesses, followed by a thorough interview about his relationships with Grant, Dobson and the Acourt brothers, his movements on the night and his purported alibi, which turned out to be false. Instead, his perfunctory statement to

Davidson was accepted and he was even afforded an alias, Witness K. Aliases are normally reserved for those who have provided crucial information and require protection.

On top of all this, it now appears that Mr White's stepfather had contacted the police soon after the murder in order to convey information. This contact was placed on the wrong database and was not followed up for twenty years, even though it had been requested by the Kent police review and by the Macpherson Inquiry. What the stepfather had to say was explosive – his stepson had confessed to participating in the murder and had added that Stephen deserved it.

Meanwhile, when Gary Dobson was interviewed by police in the days that followed his arrest, he changed his original alibi that he was at home on the night, to accepting that he was in fact at the Acourts' address when Matthew White visited, informing them of the murder in Well Hall Road. This was something he repeated at his trial.

Even this is not the end of the story, because it lends weight to the long-standing belief the family have held, namely that the number and the magnitude of the investigative mistakes cannot possibly be matters of pure accident, coincidence or oversight. In the light of these revelations, it is hoped the Undercover Policing Inquiry will be able to shed even more light on the approach of police to this case.

The Lawrence Legacy and the Horizon

Space has been afforded here to the detailed chronicle of this struggle in the sincere hope it will inspire and not daunt the thousands of similar warriors who fight on unheralded. There can be no peace for the family – or the nation – until justice is achieved at all levels and all fronts. Stephen's family – Doreen, Neville, Stuart and Georgina – have come to realise that unless they activate others and keep the flame alight, there is unlikely to be any change.

They have taken this burden on themselves, year in and year out. Doreen in particular has assisted other families facing similar odds, such as those of the victims of Bloody Sunday and Hillsborough. She has also assisted the National Civil Rights Movement (NCRM), established in the wake of Stephen's murder by Suresh Grover, myself and others to proffer advice and support.

For his part, Neville returns from Jamaica from time to time to spread the word, especially among the younger generation. He recognises the powerful image his son has left – the ubiquitous photograph of Stephen in a black and white striped top against a green foliage background with his right fist clenched. No words are needed, it is synonymous with resistance and hope. I met Neville at the Race and Equalities Council offices in Southwest London. He works with the organisation, touring the country to create a better understanding of inbred prejudice. They have visited sports clubs, particularly football, tackled knife crime, addressed young offenders and attended a hate crime conference at Essex police headquarters in Chelmsford. This is not a man who has let his grip slip for one minute.

When I asked him what has kept him going through thick and thin, his answer was not unexpected but it had an inner story that I had not been aware of before. The memory of his son is naturally the central force, but that is amplified by his own upbringing. He was brought up in Jamaica by his grandmother. There's nothing unusual in that, except she was white, with a Jewish background in pre-war Germany. Until he was 8 or 9, Neville thought she was his mother – 'It's part of the culture not to ask questions'. He realised later that assimilating and processing such dramatic information strengthened his own feelings of responsibility about parenthood and Stephen.

This year – 2023 – marked the 30th anniversary of the murder. The memorial was held at St Martin-in-the-Fields in Central London, just like previous memorials. The last memorial was supposed to be the final one. Doreen did not want to have to convene another. But the spectacle of gross misconduct by police and those in government over the recent past compelled her to take up the baton again. Once more, she brought together those in power to face the force of the people. The new Commissioner of the Met sat alongside Doreen and Stuart. The leader of the opposition, Sir Keir Starmer, and Mayor of London, Sadiq Khan, were just across the aisle. There was a space reserved for the Prime Minister, Rishi Sunak, who was due to read from Nelson Mandela's *Long Walk to Freedom*. But he did not appear, nor did he appoint a colleague to take his place, nor was any message conveyed to the congregation, nor to the public. But perhaps that was the message.

Chapter 5
Silence is Not an Option

Silence is Not an Option is the title of a book written by Sukhdev Reel, the story of yet another mother, another son, another murder. And yet again the pervasive obduracy of racism and authority, and the unrelenting struggle for truth, accountability and change. Still, however, this dreadful wrong has not been resolved, but this has by no means dampened the resolution of the people in pursuit.

This murder occurred in 1997 in Southwest London, the same year as the tide-turning moments in the Lawrence story. Sukhdev's son Ricky went for a night out in Kingston upon Thames with three Asian friends. Like Stephen, he never returned home after a racist attack.

Prising open the evidential closets and closed minds around this terrible death has taken a spectacular effort by Sukhdev and her family, especially at the inquest where I represented her, instructed by the dedicated solicitor Louise Christian.

You can still see the impact it has had on her today. Sukhdev sits on a sofa in her living room, talking to her young grandchild. The inexorable bond between them is evident. She smiles as the child leaves the room, but that smile fades as she begins to talk. 'On 14 October 1997 Ricky and his three Asian friends went out to a Kingston nightclub. They parked the car in Down Hall Road in Kingston. The police car passed by, and they asked directions to the nightclub. As they were walking, two white men started shouting racist abuse. There was a fight. Ricky was saying that he wanted to be home by 1am. And he had an urgent conference that he wanted to attend the next morning.

'When he did not come home at 1am, I didn't know where he was. I was panicking, his mobile was switched off. I started to ring nearby police stations and hospitals. I wasn't getting anywhere. I thought they might have been involved in a car accident. This continued all night long. I phoned the local police station and asked if they could come and take a statement, my son is missing. They said no, you have to wait for 24 hours and if Ricky does not come home then, to make another call. I waited and I was pleading with the police. I said this is not like Ricky to go away without telling me, he always returns when he says he will. I waited for the police to arrive. I phoned them again, the police officer started shouting at me. They said the police had come but I refused to answer the door. This was wrong. By the time police arrived I had called Brunel University to see about any other friends who may have information.

'The police officer came, apologised – he had been given the wrong address. He phoned Brunel University; the friends told the police officer that they had been racially abused and attacked by two white men. The police officer refused to take a statement, even though he was the one who told me of the racial attack. He said wait for 24 hours and if he doesn't come then come back to us.

'We then went to Kingston police station with Ricky's friends, who showed us where the car park was, they showed us where they were attacked. Instead of taking a statement, the police said, "You Asian people are all arranging marriages, maybe he's run away, or maybe he is gay, or he did not want to return home." This was within the first 24 hours.

'That's when I started to raise my voice. We knew we were not going to get any support or assistance from the police. For seven days we were out on the streets – posters, cameras, locating CCTV, speaking to people, we did all of the investigation that the police should have done. Kingston was deserted at night time, we jumped into bins, climbed into late night buses. People were very angry, why are you doing this, why aren't the police doing it? The police were not there to support us. We did not see a police officer in Kingston for a whole week.'

Ricky was found in the river a week later. The news was imparted to the family in a brusque and upsetting manner by police, creating real anguish for Sukhdev and her young children. This was compounded by an almost immediate, simplistic assumption being peddled by senior officers as conclusive, namely that Ricky went to the river to urinate and fell in. Case closed. A complaint was lodged for another force to take over, but the Met claimed it was not closed. In their minds, however, it certainly was. An investigative stalemate and stagnancy. The Police Complaints Authority (PCA) therefore appointed the Surrey force – not to investigate the event but only the complaint about how the Met had handled it!

From that very moment onwards, Sukhdev determined to counter the assumption and was tireless in setting up the Justice for Ricky Reel Campaign and enlisting the support of a broad range of individuals and groups, such as Southall Monitoring Group and Suresh Grover*, the local MP John McDonnell and over time thousands of

---

* Suresh Grover is still today a Co-Director of The Monitoring Group in London, which was established in the 1980s as Southall Monitoring Group in the wake of the killing of Blair Peach in 1979 during an anti-racist demonstration in Southall.

community workers, lawyers, journalists, musicians, writers and poets.

There was an unexpected turning point to come. The inevitable inquest had to take its course. The assumption would be put to the test.

I remember 1 November 1999 at Fulham Town Hall as clearly as Sukhdev does. We were in front of a coroner and a jury. There was real tension in the air. I walked alongside Sukhdev who was naturally very apprehensive. The pavement outside and the corridors inside were crowded with public and press. The intransigence of the police was readily discernible from attitudes and body language. Sukhdev's persistence was not appreciated, and there was tangible but unspoken hostility to such an extent that Sukhdev's brother, as well as Suresh Grover and others were excluded from the hearing.

I always believe that you must know the scene of the incident, or the 'locus in quo' as it is termed. So I had walked every conceivable route in Kingston, retracing Ricky's steps, examining the spot alleged to be where Ricky might have fallen in the river, noting the positions of CCTV cameras, the nightclub, the car park, the bus stop and so on. I had spent time getting to know the family, their feelings of anguish and anger, and their strong sense of justice. So much so that we have remained friends. I take the view that those you represent need to know where possible that you have mastered and understood their predicament. It is the best form of reassurance you can provide. You must be able, in a sense, to stand in their shoes. There were burning questions to be asked, which suggested that Ricky's death was not an accident.

Before the court sat in the main semicircular council chamber, I had a message that the coroner, Dr John Burton, wished to see me in his room. I am customarily somewhat hesitant about such invitations and in a criminal case would not accept one without counsel for other parties being present. Inquests, however, are not trials and have a protocol of their own. I had appeared in front of him before* and, as was well known, he was idiosyncratic in demeanour and outspoken in his opinions. I certainly had no wish to get off on the wrong foot. He was pouring tea from a Thermos and offered me a cup. My recollection is that, circuitously, he wanted to know what stance I was adopting on behalf of the family in terms of issues and whether there might be any problems in the public gallery. The general stance of the family was already in the public domain, so I did not really think that was his purpose, and the campaign was hardly a secret. I thought to myself that it was probably a thinly disguised attempt to discover how things were

---

* During the *Marchioness* case (see Chapter 8, page 121).

going to pan out, to forestall any troublesome areas and keep matters – or me! – on an even keel. I took the opportunity to make clear that the restriction of access to the public gallery was not acceptable and I would wish to raise the matter in public.

It was a hard-fought inquest. We made a string of serious criticisms about the numerous investigative failures to gather evidence expeditiously and thoroughly – the CCTV, witnesses (especially a bus driver and the three friends) and scientific site evidence, as well as a failure to mount a reconstruction to jog the memories of anyone around that night.

Much of this failure could be attributed to the key senior officer, Detective Superintendent Charles 'Bob' Moffat, whose first contact with the family Sukhdev remembers 'as a consultant from the police, didn't explain his role, but then said he was going on holiday for a few days'. It was this officer who perpetuated the accident theory; it was this officer who authorised a second postmortem without the knowledge or consent of the family, in which skin was removed from Ricky; it was this officer who was heavily criticised in the PCA report for lack of leadership and took early retirement.

At the inquest, another officer – Sue Hill – took over but maintained the same position, namely that it was an accident. Sukhdev gave evidence, but the coroner seemed more interested in her participation in the Stephen Lawrence Inquiry. She'd been asked to give evidence at the second stage, when the inquiry was examining how other racist incidents were handled.

The jury returned an open verdict. This was not the result the police wanted or expected. It meant they could not close the book. Accidental death was the verdict left by the coroner for the consideration of the jury, but the jury found there was insufficient evidence for it. This provided a much-needed boost and building block for the family's mission for truth and accountability.

From there on in, the way forward was peppered with obstruction and endless meetings. The PCA report had to be dragged out of the police, and was not available at the time of the inquest. John McDonnell MP raised its unavailability in the Commons. The reticence can no doubt be explained by its heavily critical contents about the investigation and dealings with the family.

On 11 January 2023, 26 years after Ricky's death, the Commissioner of the Metropolitan Police, Sir Mark Rowley, agreed to meet Sukhdev and reopen the investigation, which had remained dormant over the years. This had happened before, in October 1998, when a previous Commissioner, Sir Paul Condon, did the same.

But maybe this time the message has percolated through the layers of habitual thinking, maybe they now realise this case will not fade away until the job that should have been done in the first place is properly addressed.

The Met put out a statement that said:

The Met's Major Inquiries Specialist Casework team has re-examined the case and is now looking more closely at certain lines of enquiry from the original investigation. These lines of enquiry are being followed up with fresh eyes and the benefit of modern technology so we can explore every possible avenue in the hope of providing answers to Ricky's family.

A lesson for all of us. Never give up. Do not let go. Have faith in the strength of your belief.

But this is only a fraction of what the family has achieved.

There are days when it has been difficult for Sukhdev to get up, days when she's had to drown her tears and cries in the shower and when the pain has been unbearable. But there was no other choice – 'I must get up and get justice for Ricky'. The force cannot be stopped, nor satisfied in any other way.

En route to the current reinvestigation, Sukhdev has influenced many important reforms, which she explained to me. 'The MISSING PERSONS guidelines – if a person was over 18, they wouldn't do anything until 18 hours had passed. Now a vulnerability clause has been added to the missing persons policy – that was the policy used with Nicola Bulley*. I gave submissions to the Macpherson Inquiry – with recommendations for the family liaison officers – because of the damage they did to my children†. They should be given proper training, cultural training rather than stereotyping every Asian person who comes through their door.

'We were handing out INFORMATION to the police which we discovered they lost, or lied that they never received it, even though their logbooks confirmed that we handed the evidence in. At the inquest, they alleged that the family had not told the police things, but you kept having to point out they did. So . . . every case like this should have an INCIDENT ROOM set up. After seven days there should be a RECONSTRUCTION. They didn't do it in this case and the coroner wanted to know why, as we did, because we had to organise it ourselves.

---

* Nicola Bulley went missing in January 2023. Due to mental health issues, she was classed as 'high risk' by police, meaning they believed there was a real and immediate danger to her safety.

† Three of Sukhdev's other children were informed of Ricky's death by police officers without their parents being present.

'Twenty-five years haven't been wasted. These changes have come in not just for us, but for future generations. If I can push someone through the tunnel into the light, then my fight for Ricky is being successful.'

By writing, by speaking, by marching – by being there to be seen – the vibration is felt by the vulnerable and the governors alike.

When poet Benjamin Zephaniah (like me, a patron of the vegetarian charity Viva!) was awarded a bursary by the Poetry Society for a workplace residence, he chose my chambers – Tooks, as it was known at the time. Practice at the Bar, like so many specialisms, runs the risk of insularity and narrow vision. We can all benefit from an outside view, a different perspective, a taste of a disparate experience. Benjamin spent a year watching, listening and observing the various predicaments and struggles in the courts.

At the end, we wondered what form his collected work might take. None of us was ready for what unfolded. We were totally captivated and mesmerised. It was not a book at that stage, but an oral recitation, over two hours, of all the poems he had mentally stored from what he had witnessed. Eyes and minds were opened. Overleaf is the final stanza of a poem dedicated to Ricky, which appears in the anthology entitled *Too Black, Too Strong*.

There is a great wickedness here
And it thrives on people who do nothing,
It is planted deep in the souls of the serious sick
I don't know how to say dis,
But things are certainly not getting better,
The pacifists are out,
The militants are out
And we will not be defeated,
But it's hard, very hard.
I keep seeing your face in my self
And every time I see your mother
There is a constant
I love you Ricky
In her eyes.

Chapter 6
Pause for Thought – Transition

An underlying theme in the preceding chapters is death, one of the certainties of life. It is often these extremes that focus the mind and energise the body. Many of the instances to follow also arise from fatal circumstances. But such tragedies are not in themselves the point – it is more how they expose the dispositions and predispositions of the society within which we live. In each instance, the individuals and groups affected share a commonality of principle, a value which underpins or should underpin our 'democracy': respect for and equality before the law, otherwise described as the 'Rule of Law'. Increasingly over the last fifty years, it has become apparent that mainstream politics has become divorced from this concept to the extent that the people in power have shown little respect or regard when it comes to their own conduct.

Alongside these cases, during the same half century, there has been a steady development of various international treaties, charters, covenants and conventions on human rights enshrining these values to provide a universal consensus and infrastructure of support for the individuals and groups. Besides the UN charter, the European Convention on Human Rights (ECHR) is one of the most comprehensive. Its articles are essentially intended to protect the right to life, to freedom from torture and inhuman or degrading treatment, to a fair trial, to freedoms of association, assembly, speech, thought, expression, privacy and family life, and prevent discrimination. At this juncture it is as well to reflect upon the mother of all proclamations – the Universal Declaration of Human Rights – which was so close, as I will describe in Chapter 13, to the heart of Stéphane Hessel:

> Article 1: All human beings are born free and equal in dignity and rights. They are endowed with reason and conscience and should act towards one another in a spirit of brotherhood.

The ECHR came into force in 1953 but was not incorporated into UK domestic law until 1998, a critical year in the chronology of the cases reviewed in this book. It has made a major contribution to the rights and status of these individuals and groups, for example in the context of public inquiries, and especially inquests which are peculiar to the UK. It has placed the 'people' centre stage and empowered them, in stark contrast to my early years at the Bar in the late 1960s. Each inquest and each inquiry into the circumstances of a death now commences with a 'Pen Portrait' drawn by the family and friends. It may be on paper, spoken or filmed. The idea is to ensure that the deceased are not treated as a number, that they are brought to life for the purpose of paying due regard to their rights.

It will come as no surprise that there has been a growing cohort of reactionary 'people in power'. Their objective is to override the ECHR or even withdraw from it, to ignore decisions made by the European Court of Human Rights (for example on the issue of small boats carrying immigrants) and ultimately to construct an alternative British Bill of Rights, foreshadowed in June 2022. It will also come as no surprise that the purpose of these moves is not about the people at all but about control and, above all, power. Ironically, 'human rights' are being demeaned as part of the derogatory 'woke' culture by those in power, many of whom are themselves clothed in sleaze. The 'people' are viewed as a threat, and that takes us right back to what is at stake – truth, accountability, fairness and justice.

Enforcing and implementing these elements of the rule of law has evolved as people have recognised the need for combination and solidarity. 'Divide and rule' has been the mantra of governance for generations. They can deal with the odd rebel, but not the prospect envisaged by Percy Bysshe Shelley in the wake of the Peterloo Massacre in his poem *The Masque of Anarchy* – 'Ye are many – they are few'.

The legal process is designed to individualise, particularly in the criminal arena. In the general run of affairs, each defendant has his or her own case and representation. But the waning of deference to authority and the desire to challenge has brought families, friends and supporters together. They have gained from strength in numbers, from those with experience. Co-ordinating resources to seek evidence and to research arguments common to different individuals has led to the establishment of family groupings and campaigns, developments which could only evolve from an empowered constituency of people demanding answers. This was not a feature of the work I undertook in the 1960s, but since then it has become a natural and necessary aspect of bolstering the confidence and courage of those in the firing line. This can be as important outside as inside the court or tribunal, where the surroundings and the procedures can present an unfamiliar and daunting prospect.

Permanent support and advice organisations have established accessible, free and invaluable means of assistance – they include Inquest, Liberty (formerly the

National Council for Civil Liberties), and a national network of neighbourhood and community law centres. The first of these was set up in North Kensington in 1970, not far from the Mangrove or from Grenfell Tower. Soon after, I helped set up the second one in Tottenham, North London, now the Haringey Law Centre. The central concept was built on the idea of facilitating equal access to the law. There's not much point in having rights if you can't afford to utilise them. So, it had to be local, not forbiddingly formal or posh, akin to a familiar corner shop but, unlike the shop, free. Funding comprised a mixed basket of providers, from central and local government to voluntary donations. Recently, it's been struggling to survive, like many public services, against a backcloth of well-known austerity cuts to all publicly funded legal aid.

Alternative sources have begun to appear, dependent on the generosity of an already stretched public. The principal method is crowdfunding for a specific cause or case. It must be carefully managed and ring fenced, but has enabled important issues to be litigated. This is enhanced by international and national websites such as Avaaz and Change.org raising awareness and petitions about maladministration and injustice. They are both web movements aiming, as Avaaz says, 'to bring people-powered politics to decision-making'.

Presently, the gamut of need is vast, augmented by global forces impacting our daily lives – the recent pandemic, the energy crisis, global warming, the cost of living crisis, poverty, famine, pestilence, numerous war zones and extreme climate events such as floods, wildfires, avalanches, mudslides, drought and earthquakes. Human responsibility runs throughout, allied to a dire deficiency in national and international organs of governance. Big questions arise from all these dreadful circumstances. Was it foreseeable? Who knew? Who should have known? Was it preventable? What can be done?

It is time for the people to get the answers and reset the clock before it's too late.

Chapter 7
Safety First

All the questions posed in the last chapter have converged in three major national catastrophes, after which it has taken the people to set the agenda, as well as the clock:

The sinking of the *Marchioness*
The Hillsborough football stadium disaster
The Grenfell Tower inferno

All three have involved a variety of judicial mechanisms, the best known of which are the inquest and the judicial inquiry. I have been involved in all of them, representing some of the families and friends in each. Beyond the immediate participants, there are many more – supporters and the public – who combine to ensure that truth, accountability and justice are kept well in focus.

The core value at the heart of this process relates to respect for the right to life. A right to which only lip service had been paid prior to each catastrophe. Had it been otherwise, the likelihood of multiple deaths could almost certainly have been avoided. The factors that undermined the primacy of safety and the protection of life are not difficult to discern and remain features of our daily lives. They are potentially both corrosive and destructive.

The principal factors contributing to a fundamental disregard for the integrity of life are to be found cultured by the profit motive, the acquisition and retention of power, race and class prejudice, habitual dishonesty, incompetence, indolence, apathy and an overriding disrespect for the rule of law. Those who govern have a habit of referring to the values of our democracy not being reflected, for example, by their opponents, or by arrivals from foreign shores. These three cases have exposed the utter hypocrisy of these assertions.

A common denominator for all three is that they did not occur out of the blue. There had been prior collisions on the same stretch of the River Thames as the *Marchioness* disaster; prior overcrowding at the Leppings Lane end of the Hillsborough football ground in Sheffield; and prior warnings about an inferno of exactly these proportions by the residents of the Grenfell Tower. None had been taken seriously and no precautionary safeguarding measures had been put in place. In one sense, these were catastrophes waiting to happen. The explanation, however, never resides in a single reason but can be identified in a readily recognisable combination of the interrelated motives already listed above.

At the time of writing, it is not known exactly when the Grenfell Inquiry report will be published (probably early 2024) and it would therefore not be appropriate nor permissible for me as counsel involved in the inquiry to comment on witnesses or pre-empt any detailed conclusions, especially relating to attribution of cause or responsibility. There is a published interim report which is adequate for the purposes set out here, namely to spotlight the vital role of the citizen.

For me, a distinctive development in these cases was the fact that I was representing a large group rather than an individual client in the traditional manner. Why and how this has happened is a result of the progress outlined in the previous chapter. Most of the cases I took on at the start of my career related to one or two individuals as clients. The sea change occurred once citizens realised that their voice had potential and they had a right to be heard.

On the ground, this was no easy transition because such groups are not homogenous and naturally contain a cross-section of personalities and talent. There is a unity of purpose to obtain truth, accountability and justice, but how that is achieved creates heated debate. At once the different approaches leap off the page. Some want bold contention, others subtle suggestion. There are matters of style over content but, equally, the scope and substance of the content can be controversial. Legal issues must be canvassed and understood, especially where they bear upon the admissibility of evidence, anonymity of witnesses or grants of immunity from prosecution.

The scale of these developments is augmented by a further dimension. The clients are nearly always given essential assistance by a support network, which is often formalised into a campaign, occasionally more than one. An important distinction must be drawn to prevent compromise. As counsel I represent the client, family or friend and not the campaign. This is not an easy boundary to sustain because the client may wish a campaign member to accompany them, or the campaign may wish to publicise matters that traverse a point of law or a confidence. In these circumstances, it is vital for clear lines of demarcation to be explained and a spirit of co-operation to be fostered. Meetings, unlike legal conferences, can run to hundreds of people and cannot be underestimated.

Besides the innumerable conferences and meetings to ensure inclusivity and understanding prior to the hearings themselves, once you get to the courtroom it is even more complex. There has to be provision for large confidential conferences (for clients, not the campaign), welfare support, adequate and accessible seating in the court, basic refreshment facilities. The Coroner's Court system dates back to the 11th century, just after the Norman Conquest. Many of the buildings, while not that old, were built during the Victorian era and some are Grade II listed (for example, St Pancras just north of the station in London). They are chapel-like in dimension and hold very few people.

As both inquests and inquiries have expanded in number and size over the last fifty years, larger buildings have been used – mostly town halls like Fulham and the old Greater London Council Chamber. But because of dual use, even these cannot cope. Specialised buildings are now being established. Whereas the *Marchioness* Inquest was held in Hammersmith Council Chamber, the subsequent inquiry was at the Central Hall, Westminster. The Hillsborough Inquests were held in a converted warehouse in a business park near Warrington in Cheshire. The Grenfell Inquiry was held in a converted premises near Paddington Station in London, as is the current Covid Inquiry.

Keeping tabs on all the evidence, live, delivered either from the witness box or remotely – and the thousands of computerised documents – is a major challenge for everyone, especially when hearings can take not just months, but years. Not everyone has access to a computer and even if they do, working out the platforms being utilised is not straightforward (include me in that!). Not everyone can attend each day. Not everyone speaks the language. Not everyone is of able body and mind. Co-ordination and communication therefore must be maintained at the highest level, and this requires extensive support and advice.

All this is very different from the legal landscape back in 1967 when I started. It is critical that the progress so far achieved by ordinary people being able to ask the questions and challenge the assumptions of authority is not submerged by unfair restrictions. Restrictions are now being increasingly placed on representation and funding and, more seriously, even on the ability to ask the questions in person. The 2005 statute primarily places this ability upon counsel to the inquiry and not counsel for the families.

Initially, the powers the Act devolved upon government to control inquiries – their scope, and what can be subject to disclosure – were a response to the scrutiny the Blair Government received in the Hutton Inquiry in 2003 (into the death of Dr David Kelly) and the subsequent 2004 Butler Review of Intelligence on Weapons of Mass Destruction.

Since then, government has become increasingly concerned about the ramifications of wide-ranging inquiries upon its own credibility. Close on the heels of the Bloody Sunday Report in 2010 came the damning Iraq War Inquiry report by Sir John Chilcot*, which had been forced by the pressure of public opinion, in particular that of the veterans. It revealed the disgraceful extent to which the public had been misled, essentially about the threat itself. Being misled by those in power is a cry that has echoed down the corridors of Westminster since it was built, and still is today, following the resignation of Boris Johnson as an MP on 9 June 2023.

It is therefore of special current interest to see how these tensions play out in the judicial inquiry being undertaken by Baroness Heather Hallett into the Covid pandemic.

---

* The hearings took place between 2009 and 2011 and the report was published in 2016.

Chapter 8
The *Marchioness* Disaster

I have lived by the River Thames, travelled to work on the river bus, partied and dined on the river, celebrated birthdays, cycled home alongside it – past all the places central to this deadly drama.

At night, the fast-flowing chilly waters, shrouded in dark shadows, present a forbidding prospect.

Unlike the embankments on either side, there is no illumination on the river itself, save that reflected from the shore or from vessels on the water. Without due care and attention, it presents a perilous navigational path at the best of times.

The *Marchioness* was a sight to behold. An 'historic' pleasure craft, originally built in the 1920s, volunteered into service to save lives at Dunkirk in WW2, and on a summer night in August 1989 hired to host a 26th birthday party for well over a hundred guests. It set sail at 1.15am from Charing Cross Pier in Central London, heading downstream towards Docklands. Many guests were on deck admiring the city skyline, others below deck relaxing. They had barely progressed beyond Southwark Bridge when the *Marchioness* was struck, twice, from the stern – in essence 'run over' by a much larger vessel.

The *Bowbelle* – not the most apposite name for an 80m- (260ft-) long suction dredger making its way from Nine Elms, Battersea, to the Shipwash bank aggregate dredging grounds off the coast of Suffolk. Throughout the subsequent legal proceedings, I would characterise this vessel as a juggernaut. Because of its size and commercial demands, there were limited tidal windows for sailing. It collided with the stern of the *Marchioness*, rolling it over and turning it further into its own path, then consequently continued to push it under the water. The anchor of the *Bowbelle* sheared through the upper deck. Those below deck were trapped.

Fifty-one died. The relatives and friends of those who died and also of those who survived combined and became the Marchioness Action Group. We all owe a great deal to the fortitude of these citizens who brought about substantial and enduring improvement to river safety, not just on the Thames, but on the many tracts of water throughout our land. Change was brought about by their initiative, their pressure, knocking on endless doors – not the prescience of government and the Ministry of Transport, nor the Port of London Authority, let alone the corporate entities. Without this pressure, barely a little finger of authority would have been lifted, and the status quo would have become encrusted in apathy.

These are the key dates:

20 August 1989	• *Marchioness* involved in River Thames collision – 51 deaths • Marine Accident Investigation Board (MAIB) initiated
1991	• Henderson (Captain) faced a criminal charge for look-out failure • Two trials – jury disagrees • MAIB investigation
June 1992	• Private prosecution brought by Ivor Glogg who lost his wife – unsuccessful due to insufficient evidence of causation and knowledge by corporate directors
July 1992	• Coroner Dr Knapman refuses to resume inquest adjourned from 1990
Jan 1993–June 1994	• Litigation in High Court alleging bias by coroner, who described family litigant as 'unhinged' • Dr Knapman replaced

Mar–April 1995	• Inquest in front of Dr Burton and a jury
	• Verdict – unlawful killing AND safety recommendations
26 July 1996	• Crown Prosecution Service: no further criminal charges
1999	• Deputy Prime Minister John Prescott announces an inquiry into safety on the Thames
22 Dec 1999	• Lord Justice Clarke report – 44 recommendations
14 Feb 2000	• John Prescott announces Public Judicial Inquiry by Lord Justice Clarke into the circumstances of the *Marchioness* disaster and its causes
2001	• Report of inquiry published

This sequence has been set out in a little detail to demonstrate again that, even in the face of massive odds and hurdles spread over years, sheer tenacious persistence and unswerving dedication to principle can ultimately shift and change attitudes and outcomes for the benefit of a much wider constituency. At each stage, Louise Christian was my instructing solicitor, as she was in the Reel case. She co-ordinated the varying spirits and inspired confidence and unity. Summarising outcomes in this way does not do them justice, but I do so in order to let the voice of a family member, Lawrence Dallaglio, retell the struggle in his own words.

The main milestones for the families were:

1. Removing the original coroner, Dr Paul Knapman, whose words and actions were beyond the pale.
2. Obtaining an 'unlawful killing' verdict by the jury, combined with pertinent recommendations.
3. Securing inquiries into the disaster itself, river safety, and the process of personal identification.
4. Ensuring a raft of far-reaching recommendations for the future (the principal ones cited below).

These were great achievements given that, straight after the sinking and loss of life, the possibility of an inquiry was rejected. The non-public, non-inclusive (basically internal) MAIB investigation was considered to be sufficient. That is how it might have been left. But they had not bargained for the likes of Eileen Dallaglio. Her son, Lawrence, sits in his study to be interviewed for this book.

His smiling wife, in dungarees, gently opens the door and slides a cup of hot tea in front of him.

'My mother Eileen came from a working-class background, they ran a sweet shop in Bethnal Green . . . she has always had this desire to strive for better and more. My sister [Francesca, 19, who was on the *Marchioness* and did not survive] got a scholarship for ballet and I went to Ampleforth College. Ironically, in trying to open doors for us, she found that the very doors she opened then slammed in her face after the disaster.

'I remember the incident very well. I was 16 years old. I was about to go on the same boat party but decided for some reason to turn it down. Mum woke me up the next day and told me the *Marchioness* had sunk. The reality to me was that my sister had obviously perished. Our world was blown apart, my parents were going in different directions. We had a very difficult couple of years. My father had a heart attack. My mum was plunged into that stage of grief . . . But once the anger subsided, the desire to do something emerged – she was an air stewardess – safety was so important.'

The *Bowbelle* was built in 1964 for British Dredging and was subsequently acquired by Ready Mix Concrete (RMC), also situated in Battersea. RMC in turn established East Coast Aggregate (ECA), then South Coast Shipping (SCS), to run and operate the Bow fleet.

Important to the case is the fact that the disaster occurred at the time of Margaret Thatcher's government. Cecil Parkinson was her Minister of Transport and, incredibly, he was on the board of RMC. The likelihood of a public inquiry was nonexistent.

'When RMC should have been attending to the grief of the 51 who died, they were celebrating £65m in profits . . . my mother bought a couple of shares in RMC and went to a couple of AGMs. She got up to speak. It was a very brave thing to do. They held their heads in shame. It took six years to get a public inquiry, a change of government and a lot of strong campaigning. Nothing is ever going to bring Francesca back. My mother was driven by the thought that no other parent should ever have to go through that.

'What drove her? It was the pain and the injustice. There is nothing worse than burying your own child. The coroner severed the hands of the victims without asking the permission of the parents. This really affected my mum on many levels. Not just for herself but for others.'

This extraordinary act was the most macabre and inhumane decision by the coroner, Dr Paul Knapman. Dr Knapman authorised it for 27 of the deceased and was reluctant to attend a subsequent inquiry. Not surprising because the rationale – that it was for the purpose of identification by fingerprints – did not bear scrutiny. It explains why relatives were denied access at the time to identify their loved ones, despite the traumatic circumstances. But they were not told the truth, nor had they given consent.

As Lawrence points out, 'The rescue boats were sent in the wrong direction, the [*Bowbelle*] captain was intoxicated, there wasn't a look out – it was unlawful killing.'

It certainly was. Just by looking at the size of the Bow vessel, it was obvious. It was completely out of place on the river. A mammoth ploughing through the most crowded section of river. A juggernaut weighing approximately 1,500 tons, doing an average speed of 8.5 knots, with no possibility of slamming on the brakes if something suddenly crossed its path. You would think somebody might have realised that being behind the wheel of such an unwieldy monster would require maximum visibility and precision steering, particularly on an unlit river at night.

The ship's bridge, where the steering was managed, however, was positioned in the least advantageous place, nestling low in the stern. Depending on ballast, and on deck plant required for dredging, the chances of a clear and uninterrupted view ahead down the massive length of deck, let alone beyond, were minimal.

You would think somebody might have changed all that since there had been previous incidents on the river with the Bow fleet. Instead of raising the wheelhouse and/or employing the latest navigational aids, it was decided to use the well-worn method from the early days of the motor car, namely a man with a flag. This man, or even two, would stand up on the foredeck of the bow and either wave or, better still, blow a whistle should an obstacle appear. Provided of course the captain and others had not had too much to drink. It's beginning to sound like a circus act, you may think.

The families got it. The jury got it. Gross negligence manslaughter. How come none of the authorities had got it before the fatal day and taken precautionary measures? It's too easy to attribute it to a shortage of common sense. These guys in authority are well endowed with that.

But it's more fundamental. They don't want to know, their interests lying only in power or money – or both, without having to earn either.

Precautions are boring, expensive and get in the way. The little people won't notice anyway. And if by chance they do, we will blame someone else. This veritable merry-go-round of buck-passing would be later spelled out in full in the Grenfell Tower Inquiry.

After the collision, the *Bowbelle* was sold abroad, renamed and, in 1996, split in half at sea off the island of Madeira.

There is an eerie YouTube film of its watery grave, showing the deadly wheelhouse and the killer anchor. That's where it should have been in the first place.

The personal impact for Lawrence Dallaglio himself was life changing. 'I didn't want to take up rugby. I needed to sort my shit out. I needed a sense of purpose, a sense of belonging. When I joined the club in 1990, I had a real purpose; it was to honour the memory of my sister really. I was driven by something, and it was much more powerful than anything. My mother's crusade and the action group – she was a force of nature – I am a big believer in the power of the human spirit.'

Lawrence later captained the England rugby team and is one of the most celebrated players ever in the game. That same spirit to which Lawrence refers filled the Central Hall, Westminster towards the end of the inquiry. Final submissions had been made to Lord Justice Clarke by all the lawyers, but Eileen wanted to add some words of her own. This was not something contemplated by the rules but, as a matter of judicial discretion, I hoped this might be permitted. The Lord Justice who had presided with great care and consideration acceded to my request for Eileen to speak.

'As we approach the twelfth Christmas without our children, our brothers and sisters, our family and friends, we ask this investigation to begin the process of fundamental change in legislation, which still allows the sector of corporate greed to overshadow responsibility and accountability. Never again must companies such as RMC, ECA, SCS and Tidal Cruisers be allowed to operate their vessels along English waters and the high seas with complete and utter disregard for the safety of the general public at large. Never again must companies be allowed to fail us, the general public, by allowing inexperienced personnel with substandard intelligence, inherent drink problems, forged certificates, thereby perverting the course of justice over eleven years with total disregard for the safe operation of their vessels. Never again must managing directors appoint themselves designated safety officers without any experience of such matters. They have to know that they will be held accountable, both in criminal and civil law.'

A stunned stillness hung over the hall. It was delivered in almost Churchillian style. Egregious conduct brought down by excoriating words.

The most remarkable aspect now, for me, is that this speech – with a few tweaks – could equally have been delivered at the end of the Grenfell Inquiry last year, dealing with fire safety. It concerns a mindset and culture of indifference that must be roundly consigned to history.

The principal legacy of change resulting from the *Marchioness* disaster and the subsequent campaign for justice was multifarious. If you'll forgive another list, the changes brought about were:

1. The Corporate Manslaughter Act and Corporate Homicide Act 2007.
2. Mandatory passenger manifests for charter sailings, so it is known how many and who are on board.
3. Safety instructions and demonstration to passengers (a cause close to Eileen's heart from her airline experience).
4. Mandatory limits for alcohol and drugs for operational staff.
5. Riverbank safety equipment – grab chains and shore-side lifebuoys/belts installed. The latter faced opposition on the grounds of cost and risk of vandalism, arguments which resurfaced in Grenfell with regard to the provision of fire extinguishers, domestic or communal.
6. Lifeboat stations – one of the most obvious needs. There were none before the sinking. Now there are five in regular use on this stretch of river (one is the busiest in the UK). The RNLI search and rescue service is plainly essential, not only in terms of practised and co-ordinated rescue plans but also the deployment of specialised and

dedicated rescue craft designed to lift people out of the water. The sides of ordinary river boats and even rowing boats are too high.

7. Formulation of Metropolitan Police contingency plans.

8. A river traffic control system, similar to air traffic control, plus adequate look-out facilities on vessels.

9. Coronial system reforms – the certification and investigation of deaths was outdated and was subject to a major review in 2003.

A very fine bucket list of outcomes, thanks to you, Eileen, and all those who fought alongside you, whom I got to know so well. I will leave it to Lawrence to bring the chapter to a close.

'When you are born and bred in London, you care passionately about your home town. The motives of people like my mother should not be questioned in any way. She wasn't after compensation. She was just after justice, and justice in the sense that bad things will happen to people, we need to mitigate them and limit the possibility of them happening in the future. The legacy of the case that Michael and the victims brought is there, in terms of where it stands legally, but of equal importance is that hopefully that doesn't have to be passed on to the next generation. Ultimately the river is a safer place.'

Chapter 9
Hillsborough – Truth to Power

In 1989, on the morning of 15 April (a few months before the *Marchioness* disaster), Jenni and Trevor Hicks travelled from London to Hillsborough, together with their two daughters Sarah (19) and Vicki (15), to watch Liverpool play Nottingham Forest in the semifinal of the FA Cup. That night they drove back alone.

Ninety-six people died (now 97), the majority crushed to death. Twenty-two of them were under the age of eighteen; 760 others were injured. The two sisters were among those crushed to death. The added horror for their parents was to be present, to be witnesses – Trevor at ground level at the Leppings Lane end where the sisters had been ushered into the standing area pens, and Jenni sitting in the next stand (North) overlooking the pens. The sisters had insisted she take the seat because her height would have precluded a decent view if she were to stand.

As it turned out, their insistence saved her life – and ultimately changed it, forever.

We met some twenty years later at a critical stage in the tortuous efforts made over the whole of that time by her and many others, to uncover the truth that had been deliberately hidden. They had encountered vicissitudes and obstacles galore and were hanging onto hope by their fingernails.

Jenni came to my chambers in London, together with Margaret Aspinall, almost on spec. I took the view it was exploratory and primarily did not involve litigation but campaigning. They were both worried that an independent review which had been taking place and was about to report on the disaster might lead nowhere. In this business, you never know what's round the corner and it's never wise to jump the gun. Help often arrives from different and unexpected directions, sometimes disguised as something quite different. My advice was to stay firm, hold your breath and deal with whatever it is when it really happens. You have come this far with consummate courage.

I like to think I am an optimist and a positivist. I'm still around, so that's not a bad start.

The report they awaited was duly published in September 2012. The Hillsborough Independent Panel

(HIP) was a model of investigation and became the crucible of change. Without it, there would have been no fresh inquests, no truth and no accountability of any kind.

Getting to that stage in 2012 had been the result of relentless pressure from the families – then the people, the public at large. It had become a tidal wave that could not be resisted.

That wave had been provoked by an immense lie, perpetrated by police on the day. Liverpool fans were to blame; ticketless, drunk late-comers had forced open the gates at the Leppings Lane end and pushed their way into the crowded central Pens 3 and 4. They were responsible, therefore, for killing their own supporters. It was swiftly adopted by Tory politicians under Margaret Thatcher, who wasted no time in rushing to the scene with her Press Secretary Bernard Ingham, to show support for South Yorkshire Police. This was perhaps a repayment for the way they had carried out the Thatcher plans to disempower the National Union of Mineworkers (NUM), and particularly Arthur Scargill, during the strike in 1984. Thatcher had politicised and militarised the police as agents of her policies[*]. There was also another motive. In the 1980s, Liverpool was regarded as a den of Militant tendency, of Trots and troublemakers.

---

[*] As shown in her plan for policing Orgreave during the miners' strike. This is discussed in more detail in the Epilogue, page 260.

The inference was clear – troublesome, drunken fans from a troublesome city caused their own deaths.

This reputational smear campaign had huge repercussions which still linger right through to the present, both spoken and unspoken. The problem is that refutation gives the lie more oxygen.

It was compounded by despicable headlines in a tabloid newspaper, the *Sun*. Under the banner 'The Truth' the fans were demonised and criminalised. 'They picked pockets of the victims; they urinated on brave cops; they beat up PC giving kiss of life.' Bitter battle lines were drawn. The families had to battle grief, loss, personal humiliation, abuse and denigration.

Jenni told me, 'It wasn't just me and my grief. There were 96 families who had lost loved ones. Most recently, we lost Andrew Devine who died from the injuries he sustained 33 years ago. When a coroner ruled that he was unlawfully killed, he became the 97th victim. When you are in a campaign, the stage of the grief you are at is almost put on hold because it becomes about getting to the truth of how your loved one died, especially when you know there have been lies and corruption. It started on the day of the disaster. Not only were we grieving, but we knew something very wrong had happened.'

Meanwhile, Lord Justice Taylor held a swift and exemplary inquiry into the disaster to make interim recommendations for safety ahead of the following football season. This was the genesis of all-seater stadiums (a provision which is sadly being eroded now in favour of safe standing, which I personally regard as a contradiction in terms – do I detect a hint of the profit motive?). It is worth noting in passing that the Lord Justice was highly critical of the state of apathy and lethargy about safety matters, and the decisions made by the match-day police commander, David Duckenfield. Not to close the central tunnel gate which led to the central pens was a 'blunder of the first magnitude'.

But then came the indignity of mini-inquests, which were perfunctory and returned verdicts of accidental death. As Jenni said, 'At our first inquest, forty-odd of the families all clubbed together and all we could afford was a junior barrister. Under the circumstances he did a very good job. He ended up having to face twelve of the top QCs and their whole team.'

There was no legal aid or public funding as a rule for families at inquests. Occasionally, in exceptional circumstances, there might be an ex-gratia payment from the Lord Chancellor's department. Quite incredibly, the common argument against funding ran along the lines of: what's the point, the central figure is dead! Today it is a little easier but not automatic. The second inquests were publicly funded.

Close on the heels of these proceedings came an announcement by the Director of Public Prosecutions that no one in authority would be prosecuted. Thereafter, as recounted by Jenni, it was one rebuff after another.

A welcome moment of progress, Jenni recalls light-heartedly, came with a visit to see Jimmy McGovern*, an acclaimed local screenwriter and producer. She met him outside his house on the pretext of taking a friend's dog for a walk! The result was game changing – a BAFTA award-winning film about Hillsborough starring Ricky Tomlinson and broadcast in December 1996. The message about what really happened was spreading beyond Merseyside and galvanising calls for another inquiry. The role and impact of the film was similar to the one about the Birmingham Six by World in Action.

In 1997, a High Court judge was appointed to subject the Hillsborough investigations to a review – termed 'scrutiny' – which inspired no confidence when the reviewer, Lord Justice Stuart-Smith, commented during a

---

* Jimmy McGovern was best known at the time for creating *Cracker*, a crime drama series starring Robbie Coltrane.

meeting with a family member, 'Have you got a few of your people or are they like Liverpool fans and turn up late?' It came as no surprise that he saw no need to recommend an inquiry of any kind and no basis for an application for a fresh inquest. A stark and familiar rebuff.

Instead, the families endeavoured to mount a private prosecution against the senior officer on duty at the ground, who was responsible for the gates and the flow of fans: Chief Superintendent David Duckenfield. To get such a move off the ground, they organised a concert.

'We had the Hillsborough Justice Concert where we raised £500,000,' Jenni explained. 'We are just ordinary people; we didn't have that sort of money. They came back as a hung jury. It hung on the fact if Duckenfield was found guilty it would affect how the emergency services would react. And they would be concerned about the consequences to them.'

The jury could not agree on the various charges of manslaughter, misconduct in public office and perverting the course of justice against Duckenfield. A second defendant was acquitted.

This was a bleak and despondent point. They were empty-handed after twenty years of hard work. But from this void, there arose an unexpected voice – a voice that turned a page, and in turn would yield further unexpected results.

★

The year 2009 marked the 20th anniversary of the disaster. Each year, a service of commemoration was held at Anfield, the home ground of Liverpool FC. I attended myself in later years. 'You'll Never Walk Alone' struck a chord every time; 96 balloons would slowly drift above the ground and 96 red roses would lie side by side on the green turf of Anfield below. By this time, Andy Burnham MP (a scouser and now Mayor of Manchester) was Secretary of State for Culture, Media and Sport and had been invited to speak in front of the record-breaking 30,000 people there. He was introduced by Trevor Hicks.

Andy Burnham began by describing the gravity of the occasion, especially as it affected the younger generation. He soon found that what he was saying was not falling on totally receptive ears! When he got to a passage about a pledge from the Prime Minister, Gordon Brown, that the 96 should never be forgotten, the atmosphere changed. Rustling in the crowd and audible discontent – twenty years of frustration erupted, as a lone voice shouted, 'Justice for the 96!' Mass singing broke out with thousands standing as one voice. The city had had enough of promises and fine words; justice delayed is justice denied.

The moment was electric and can still be watched on YouTube. Anyone reading this who feels fatigued, finished, at the bottom, at an end, or convinced there is nothing that can be done to bring about change should just watch these transformative moments – it takes only a few minutes.

Jenni explained, 'At the time when Andy first took the message back to Parliament – Justice for the 96 – it was a pivotal moment . . . Andy had a good relationship with Gordon Brown and after the executive met with Lord Wills, Gordon Brown gave the go-ahead for the HIP.'

There was a cabinet meeting the next day and Gordon Brown allowed Andy Burnham to put the 96 on the agenda. This led to the establishment of the HIP to enable disclosure of all the Hillsborough documentation for scrutiny. The panel comprised seven specialists: an archivist, a researcher, a criminologist, a former Deputy Chief Constable, a broadcaster, a former Associate Medical Director at the Department of Health, and a public information expert. Pandora's box was opened at last. It was a novel venture and should be considered as a model for future reinvestigations and reviews[*].

---

[*]   A good example would be Orgreave, where no single police officer has ever been disciplined, let alone prosecuted, for fabrication or excessive force – see the Epilogue, page 260.

The chair was the Right Reverend James Jones, Bishop of Liverpool and, unusually, the publication of the report took place in the Anglican Cathedral in Liverpool. Its impressive dimensions – steeped in neogothic design – are among the largest in the world and command respect.

The proceedings in September 2012 were handled immaculately, as might be anticipated. There had been no leaks, and no one had the slightest idea what the report might say or recommend. And just to be doubly sure, the Bishop had allocated disparate areas of the cathedral for different interests. The families were all placed in the main aisle, the press were kept apart in a side chapel and the lawyers were put in what seemed like a dungeon, but was probably the crypt! All very sensible. No one would glimpse anything until the most important people were given a thorough briefing by the panel.

Jenni and Margaret had asked if I could attend as an observer. I was happy to do so and took another member of my chambers and a long-standing solicitor friend. There was likely to be a lot of reading and analysis in a short space of time, should we be asked for our thoughts.

The tension was tangible. So much was hanging on the outcome. It was overwhelming.

In short form, the report declared there was no evidence to support the assertion that the fans were to blame; there was evidence of failures of operational police control; 164 police statements had been altered; overall, crowd safety had been compromised at all levels; the coroner's cut-off point of 3.15pm (intended to mean that each of those who died had received their fatal injuries before 3.15pm and were beyond saving after that time) was erroneous; and, worse, 41 out of the 96 might have survived.

The people's voice had hit the target. Down to business immediately.

There were two main groups of families – the Hillsborough Family Support Group (HFSG) and the Hillsborough Justice Campaign (HJC). Their aims were common, but there were a host of variations on a theme. There were also individuals who were not members of either.

The HFSG was formed right at the beginning, in July 1989. 'My ex-husband Trevor was the Chair for the first 16 years,' Jenni told me. 'A couple of years later, I joined the committee and became Secretary for the group for a few years, eventually becoming the Vice Chair in the final ten years. I was also part of an Executive Committee from 2009, together with Margaret Aspinall, Sue Roberts and Trevor. We got HIP put together. It was a full-time job. I had to give up my job because there were so many meetings – trips to London to meet with ministers, particularly with Theresa May. We had meetings with David Cameron and Lord Michael Wills.'

The groups and individuals instructed separate teams of lawyers. We all knew each other well and worked closely together to save time and money and to present as unified a position as was possible. However, as a rule, meetings and discussions were mainly kept separate. 'You can't always avoid falling out with people in the campaign,' Jenni explained. 'I fell out with a close friend in our group, there were things that we were discussing that we could not discuss with other families. We did have to keep confidences. At the end of the day, we are all individuals joined together by a huge grief, but by a huge injustice. It wasn't the grief that kept us together. One of the things about being part of a group, particularly as an officer of the group you are representing, is that it's difficult to separate the fact that you're not representing your own personal feelings. There have been times when my personal views have differed from what I was supposed to have been carrying forward, but my job was to do what people wanted. We all had the same aim: truth and accountability.'

HFSG embraced a large number of people and required a team of advocates to cover all the particular needs, as well as general points of fact and law. For example, the task of determining exactly where, when and how each fatality had been occasioned was a mammoth but highly personal need for each family. A pressing question was always in the wings – could an earlier or different intervention have saved a life? The fulcrum for our group – the boss, the strategist – was Marcia Willis Stewart from the firm Birnberg Peirce. She was subsequently awarded an honorary Queen's Counsel, now King's Counsel, status in recognition of her outstanding work.

After the report in September 2012, applications to the Attorney General for new inquests were drafted and heard by the High Court in double-quick time, within months, in December 2012. Granted.

In addition, fresh criminal investigations were begun in 2013 by Operation Resolve. The Independent Police Complaints Commission (IPCC) had the task of examining the aftermath and alleged cover-up.

By 2014, the new inquests were underway, lasting until 2016.

In sum, the families had reversed 27 years of injustice in the space of just four, two of which were consumed by the inquests themselves. No mean achievement by any standards, and none of this must be overshadowed by a lack of accountability in the subsequent criminal court proceedings.

Both the truth and the responsibility for Hillsborough are writ large in the indelible findings of the inquest jury, an astonishing and eternal verdict that can never be overturned or erased, together with an unforgettable moment of communion in English legal history.

The jury retired after 319 days (the longest jury hearing, spread over two years) of hard-fought evidential dispute between the families and principally the police authorities, Sheffield Wednesday FC management and the ambulance service. They were given directions by the coroner, Lord Justice Goldring, about the questions to be answered in a newly introduced 'narrative' verdict, as opposed to a 'short form' verdict*. There were 14 questions, and although each one is crucial, it would be burdensome to rehearse the detail of all. I have selected the key ones which, like the Penn plaque at the Old Bailey, should be set in stone at Hillsborough as a constant reminder of how the jurors steadfastly carried out their duty and arrived at their clear and careful conclusions.

It was agreed that once the jury had made their determinations, there would be a suitable interval

---

* A traditional 'verdict' given at the end of an inquest was short, for example 'accident', 'unlawful killing' or 'open'. The accepted form now is a 'narrative' verdict which customarily requires the jury to answer a series of factual questions. The answers become its findings into the four basic topics of who, when, where and how.

before they were delivered publicly, to enable the many participants who lived some distance away to be present.

At around 11am on the morning of 26 April, the Forewoman of the jury was asked to confirm the findings as they were read out. Every seat was taken in the main venue, and in the overflow buildings nearby. As she stood up, it was as though every single person had stopped breathing. Usually delivering a verdict – particularly in the criminal court – takes only a minute or two, during which time I am reluctant to look directly at the jury (as counsel, constraining your own reaction is necessary). Now it was understood that going through 14 questions would take far longer.

I was sat with other lawyers in the middle, facing the coroner. To his right was the jury. To our left was one group of families and to our right was the other, the one our team represented.

I looked away. The first question was basic and non-contentious, and answered simply – 96 people were crushed to death.

It was the next series of questions asked by the coroner that were bang at the heart of the issue:

Question 2: Preplanning for the match
Coroner: 'Was there any error or omission in police planning and preparation for the semifinal match

on 25 April 1989 which caused or contributed to the dangerous situation that developed on the day of the match?

'Was your answer, Madam, "Yes"?'

Forewoman: 'It was.'

Coroner: 'Did the jury give the following explanation: "The jury feel that there were major omissions in the 1989 operational order including: specific instructions for managing the crowds outside the Leppings Lane turnstiles; specific instructions as to how the pens were to be filled and monitored; specific instructions as to who would be responsible for the monitoring of the pens".'

Forewoman: 'That's correct.'

This format was used for all questions and the drift seemed promising.

Question 3: Policing of the match
and the situation at the turnstiles

Coroner: 'Was there any error or omission in policing on the day of the match which caused or contributed to a dangerous situation developing at the Leppings Lane (LL) turnstiles?'

Forewoman: 'Yes. The police response to the increasing crowds at LL was slow and unco-ordinated. The road closure and sweep of fans exacerbated the situation. No filter cordons were placed in LL. No contingency plans were made for the sudden arrival of a large number of fans. Attempts to close the perimeter gates were made too late.'

Even more promising. Now for the first crucial issue, even though it had been foretold in the Taylor report.

Question 4: Policing of the match
and the crush on the terrace

Coroner: 'Was there any error or omission by the commanding officers which caused or contributed to the crush on the terraces?'

Forewoman: 'Yes. Commanding officers should have ordered the closure of the central tunnel (leading to the central pens) before the opening of Gate C (perimeter into ground) was requested as Pens 3 and 4 were full. Commanding officers should have requested the number of fans still to enter the stadium after 2.30pm. Commanding officers failed to recognise that Pens 3 and 4 were at capacity before Gate C was opened.'

Question 5: The opening of the gates

The answer to this question was virtually a repeat of the answer to Question 4 above.

The questions carrying the most weight, however, were the next two. Both had been the subject of extensive discussion with the families and their lawyers in both groups in order to arrive at a consensus for consideration by the coroner and his counsel, Christina Lambert KC. Unlawful killing, or gross negligence manslaughter in this context, is not straightforward evidentially, especially when there are a number of possible contributory causes which could reduce the threshold for liability, and the standard required to meet the legal test of 'gross negligence' is high.

Question 6: Determination on the unlawful killing issue

Coroner: 'Are you satisfied so that you are sure that those who died in the disaster were unlawfully killed?'

Forewoman: 'Yes.'

The legal significance here is the standard of proof to be met. At that time, it was the criminal standard, which meant the jury had to be satisfied of guilt beyond a reasonable doubt, sometimes expressed as being 'sure'. It has since changed to the (lower) civil standard, namely a jury need only be satisfied on the balance of probabilities, sometimes expressed as being 'more likely than not'. In the inquest proceedings where Duckenfield was represented by counsel, he repeated to three different counsel, including his own, that his professional failings led to the deaths of 96 innocent men, women and children.

Not surprisingly, the families could barely contain decades of pent-up emotion, frustration and anger. But there was one more absolute killer of a question, the one-word answer to which could not be guaranteed by the thread so far, and might just detract from the answer just given to Question 6.

Question 7: The behaviour of the supporters

Coroner: 'Was there any behaviour on the part of the football supporters which caused or contributed to the dangerous situation at the LL turnstiles?'

Forewoman: 'No.'

Coroner: 'Was there any behaviour on the part of football supporters which MAY have . . .'

Forewoman: 'No.'

These emphatic and unanimous verdicts are of the 'first magnitude' and can provide no better vindication for the families. A cheer went up. Tears could be held back no longer. It was difficult to maintain order for the remaining questions, although they were of equal importance.

Question 8: Defective design construction and layout – Yes

Question 9: Failure of licensing and oversight – Yes

Question 10: Sheffield Wednesday FC failures in management – Yes

Question 11: Sheffield Wednesday FC failures on day, delay of kickoff – Yes

Question 12: Failure of architects over capacity estimates – Yes

Question 13: Emergency and police response failures – Yes

Question 14: Particular failures by South Yorkshire Metropolitan Ambulance Service – Yes

This was a premier league result: The People – 14. Those in Power – 0.

There then followed for me one of the most memorable and overwhelming moments of my professional career. Someone shouted, 'God bless the jury!' There was applause. The jury stood up, the families stood up. The coroner took his leave very discreetly. The jurors crossed the courtroom in front of me and the families did the same. They met and embraced. It was a communion of spirit that seals the case for never giving up on justice in its broadest sense.

'The families all applauded,' Jenni remembers. 'There was a feeling of euphoria in there that finally – finally – we actually thanked the jury. It was this enormous feeling of relief. When the fans were exonerated, that's when you could finally breathe. It would have been a very empty verdict without that. It would have been the wrong verdict. I wouldn't have accepted it. I burst into tears . . . I cried with relief.'

Beyond the enormity of the result itself, there was an important element at play in the Hillsborough story – the central place of citizen juries in our system, as noted earlier in the historic stand taken by the Penn jury. During the time I have been practising at the Bar, I have been a strong defender of this form of democratic justice which has the capacity to return verdicts that test the integrity of the state.

At the same time, there has also been a vociferous opposition. Its origins stem from a belief that you only qualify to pass judgement if you are a property owner, and for centuries that was the bedrock. Slowly such a criterion was abolished. What took its place was a raft of hostile arguments about inadequate education, intelligence, concentration, perversity and, ultimately, expense.

Academics argued that a reasoned verdict was fairer but was beyond the capability of the average jury member.

The Hillsborough jury demonstrated the paucity of these points. They understood the proceedings well. They grasped the principles to be applied to a more detailed verdict. They survived two years – an act of true patience and stamina. It was always thought that none of this was possible, least of all to produce an agreed form of reasoned judgement.

The legacy of Hillsborough is not just about safety and safer stadiums, top priority though this is. Although this dramatic story concerns football, it is not about football. Like the other cases in this book, it uncovers the thin surface below which a vein of misrepresentation and obduracy runs. The denials, the lies, the lack of responsibility and accountability, the absence of forthright admission and apology – each of which was exposed by the men and women on the terraces. All of this is far removed from the Seven Principles of Public Life outlined by Lord Nolan and published in 1995 by the Committee on Standards in Public Life, which spelled out the critical values those in public life should uphold – integrity, accountability, honesty and transparency among them.

Hillsborough has revived the demand for candour which is reflected in an ongoing initiative by the families' lawyers to import a statutory duty of candour as an obligation upon public bodies – the Hillsborough Law, currently supported by Andy Burnham. Additionally, the government is committed to introducing an Independent Public Advocate to act for bereaved families after a disaster to provide support and preserve documentation. This has been a particular venture close to Jenni's heart and has been assisted by both Lord Wills and me. Personally, I favour a more radical facility akin to the Hillsborough Independent Panel model on a permanent basis, but dealing with injustice on a wider front – for example, miscarriages of justice generally, misconduct in public office, violations of the rule of law.

Other work emanating from Hillsborough is still in progress. There are more reports awaited from Bishop Jones and another from the Independent Office for Police Complaints (formerly the IPCC). Vile abuse is continuing on social media and such conduct needs to be confronted. The indefatigable Louise Brookes, an active campaigner and a bereaved relative, has taken on the task of tracking down the abusers and shutting them down, ultimately by court action.

When Jenni was asked what she thought the legacy of Hillsborough was, she replied, 'I think historically my book is my personal legacy [*One Day in April*] and it's to my daughters. Not to what I've done, because any parent would have done what I have done. So that my daughters aren't just two names on a memorial somewhere. So that people who read that book get to know my daughters. Sue Johnson narrates the audio version. I went to the studio the day after Sue had been there. They wanted me to do the thank yous and to give a little introduction at the beginning. There were two young people who had been in the recording studio, a guy and a girl – they said to me, after Sue had finished the book, I felt I really knew your girls. They both cried while she was reading it. So that's my personal legacy. Anybody who chooses to buy and read my book, they will think that they know my girls, and that they know what a national scandal this has been.

'Obviously I'm 34 years down the line now, but I'm getting to know myself again, and where I'm at. I'm still involved with the campaign side of it I guess. Not in the same way, not as a group, but now as an individual. I can be an individual. I don't think I've been an individual since I went to that football match that day. I became part of a national scandal . . . somewhere my own personal life got lost in all of this. The problem is you don't think it's going to take thirty years of your life, so you put other things on hold. I became part of something far bigger than me.'

Chapter 10
Grenfell – The Tower and the Community Still Stand

A few minutes before 1am on Wednesday 14 June 2017, while most people in London were asleep, a commonplace electrical-product fire began inside a flat in the Grenfell Tower in Notting Hill. The inferno that followed would not fully burn itself out for 24 hours. The fire was rapidly transformed into an inferno by the presence of combustible materials in the façade of the building. Seventy-two people died, hundreds more were injured and rendered homeless.

It was the worst residential fire in the UK since WW2 and the Blitz, a time of terror for my parents who were on emergency duties as well as contriving corrugated iron Anderson shelters, both outside and inside our small home in Whetstone, for me and others. Despite my age, the darkness, the smells and the sounds of that time have never left me.

For those who survived the Grenfell fire, the scenes etched in the mind by the rapper Lowkey in his tribute 'Ghosts of Grenfell' carry the burden of memory.

CAVEAT: *At the time of writing, the evidence and submission stages of this monumental inquiry are over. Presently, it is at the final report stage where the evidence of both phases of inquiry are assessed by the chair and his panel, conclusions are drawn, and recommendations are made. An interim report was published at the end of Phase 1, which examined events on the night.*

There is a full and final report to come, which will examine materials, design, construction, planning, testing and certification, safety inspection, regulation, maintenance, consultation, recommendations, pathology – and individual deaths.

Given the ongoing scrutiny of this terrible incident, actual publication of the final report may not occur until after this book is first published.

So, despite voluminous commentaries in the public domain, as counsel representing some of the families, it would not be appropriate for me to make comment at this juncture on individual witnesses who gave evidence in person or in writing, let alone on attribution of responsibility for identified failings and their relationship to causation of the fire, and the causation of the deaths and injuries. These are matters for the chair and his panel, assisted by their team of counsel.

Nevertheless, I wanted to write about Grenfell because what happened there is so central to the theme of this book.

When you read about the role that the families and their supporters assumed in the struggle to discover truth, not only in the wake of the fire but before it in their daily lives, you will understand why.

The Night

The immediate cause of the fire was an electrical fault in a large fridge-freezer near the kitchen window of Flat 16 on Floor 4. Grenfell was a high-rise residential block. 'High-rise' is defined as being 18m (59ft) or over, but Grenfell was much bigger than that, standing at just over 67m (220ft) tall, with 24 storeys and 120 flats. The 23 residential floors were served with a single interior staircase and lifts. Grenfell was completed in 1974 as part of a development on the Lancaster West Estate in North Kensington, comprising the tower and three low-rise finger blocks. It was subject to a refurbishment scheme between 2012 and 2016, which introduced an exterior 'envelope' or new ventilated rainscreen insulation and cladding system, the outer element of which was an aluminium composite material (ACM) in a series of façade panels.

In practice, Grenfell Tower was a vertical village, with a vibrant, diverse community (especially from North Africa), where people looked out for their neighbours. There were a significant number of disabled people living on upper floors, as well as children. There were 297 people in the block that night; 72 died. Seventy of them were unable to escape (principally from the upper floors 11 to 23) and two died later. Almost half of those who died were either disabled or children. Of particular note, there was no general emergency evacuation plan, let alone a personalised one tailored to need.

The occupant of Flat 16 was woken up by the sound of the fire alarm in the kitchen. There was no sprinkler system inside the tower, nor on the exterior façade. There were no standard fire extinguishers in the communal areas of each floor, nor were there any domestic handheld versions in individual flats.

In the interim report, the chair pointedly observed:

Two very important matters have come to light from the evidence put before me in Phase 1:

First, that in its origin, the fire at Grenfell Tower was no more than a typical kitchen fire; second, that the fire was able to spread into the cladding as a result of the proximity of combustible materials to the kitchen windows.[1]

Concise and poignant, the interim report notes the following initial stages of the fire:

00.54 A 999 call is made from Flat 16
00.59 The fire service reaches the tower
01.09 Fire breaks out of Flat 16 into the exterior cladding and rapidly starts to climb the east façade
01.14 Firefighters enter the kitchen of Flat 16 for the first time
01.27 The fire reaches the roof and starts to spread horizontally
04.00 Fire is still evident on the south and west elevations

There are moments in all our lives when you can remember exactly where you were when you learned some singular dramatic news – perhaps the Cuban missile crisis in October 1962 or the giant leap for mankind on the moon in July 1969. Or later, the death of Princess Diana in August 1997 or the murder of George Floyd under the knee of a white police officer in May 2020. There will be many others, particularly in an age of instantaneous global communication – but one is undoubtedly the Grenfell Tower fire.

What happened on 14 June 2017 was seen by millions. Within seconds it had flashed across television screens around the world. It was a horror movie – a towering inferno – which could hardly be believed, least of all by those who had friends or relatives in the tower. That was precisely the desperate situation for some of the families I represented, one abroad in Italy, the others right here in the UK. Helpless witnesses, like the Hicks family were at Hillsborough. A struggling human silhouette against a window frame, a fatal leap from the upper floors.

It was the speed of the flames and the ubiquitous spread of acrid black smoke that was overwhelming for the residents.

The gravity and huge impact of the fire cannot be overstated nor forgotten for one moment. The lessons are for everyone and reach far beyond the mechanics of how and why the fire occurred. Just as Hillsborough was not just about football safety, Grenfell is not just about the construction of tower blocks. They both also touch on the core values which are meant to underpin a democratic society and determine the way in which our lives are governed.

As we saw in the last chapter, an attempt was made to try to set standards in relation to Hillsborough. It is instructive to recall them in the light of events over the subsequent decades, including Grenfell Tower as well as Hillsborough.

An advisory non-departmental public body had been established in 1994 – the Committee on Standards in

Public Life – chaired by Lord Nolan who was at the time a Lord of Appeal in Ordinary. A code was promulgated, which became known as the Seven Principles of Public Life, or the Nolan Principles. It was intended to apply to (a) those elected or appointed to public office, nationally or locally; (b) those appointed to work in the Civil Service, local government, the police, courts and probation services, non-departmental public bodies, and health and education, social and care services; (c) those in the private sector delivering public services. This is a comprehensive list, which encompasses all those involved in the maintenance and refurbishment of Grenfell Tower.

The seven agreed principles are: Integrity, Selflessness, Accountability, Openness, Objectivity, Honesty and, last of all, Leadership.

In contrast to these principles, there are certain stark features (which have a resonance in common with all the other cases mentioned so far) that have been readily exposed by the evidence in the two phases of the inquiry. The significance of these features is the extent to which they created a controlling mindset or culture, wherein safety was neglected, was relegated and was not a top priority. They are exemplified by ignorance, indolence, avarice, negligence, indifference, arrogance, incompetence, irresponsibility, dishonesty and politico-economic dogma.

Which individuals and which organisations manifest any or all of these characteristics and their relationship with the mindset is a matter of final determination for the inquiry. Of even greater import is the ultimate determination of the extent to which any or all of these features caused or contributed to the causes of the fire, and consequentially to the causes of the deaths and injuries.

The centrality of the families, friends and supporters is not purely as an act of remembrance and tribute, but also as an inspiration for a different future, incorporating fairness and respect. What has now become an accepted procedure, as described earlier, whether in an inquest (Hillsborough) or an inquiry (Grenfell) is the presentation of Pen Portraits. These invariably take place right at the start (for Grenfell, two weeks in May 2018). They are salutary and breathtaking. They help ensure that you do not lose sight of the real objectives concerned with justice.

A written summary of the portraits is contained in Chapter 32 of Volume 4 of the interim report, but nothing can reproduce the live testimony – the photographs, the film, the poems, the artwork. Whether it is a whole family (in two cases five or six members of a family died) or one person – a more elderly soul alone on an upper floor, or a child lost on the stairs – they all deserve the equality of a safe place to live. It is of interest to note that Grenfell

Tower was primarily social housing, as were all the many earlier examples of tower block fires in the UK provided to the inquiry*.

There are so many accounts from this apocalyptic sequence that selecting any is invidious. Among the families I represented, there are two in stark contrast on Floor 21: the El Wahabi family in Flat 182 and Ligaya Moore in Flat 181. The former was a family of five – father Abdulaziz (52), mother Faouzia (42), son Yasin (20), daughter Nur Huda (15) and youngest son Mehdi (8). Both parents were born in the same town in Morocco but had lived and worked in London for over twenty years. They were respected, jovial members of the community. Next door was Ligaya Moore (78). She lived alone, having moved to London from the Philippines in 1972 and married in the UK. Ligaya was full of energy and a keen charity worker.

They all died.

There were other members of the Wahabi family – Abdulaziz's younger sister Hanan, her husband and children lived in Flat 66 on a lower floor of the tower. They managed to evacuate and gathered outside with the agony of watching and listening to the plight of her brother's

---

* These other examples can be found conveniently narrated in a BBC documentary, *The Fires that Foretold Grenfell* (2018).

family and endeavouring to give them advice and support over a mobile phone.

At 01.25, still feeling the effects of the smoke in her chest and lungs, Hanan sent a photograph of the fire to her brother to alert him. She recalled her first call to him, 'Abdulaziz answered my call and I said to him "There's a fire". Abdulaziz said he was aware of something going on, and he kept saying, "Shall I come down? What do you think?" I said, "I think you should get out. It's on my side now, not on your side." He said, "Alright sis, I'm coming."'

Hanan could hear people screaming and see chunks of debris falling. The flames had reached the top of the tower. Hanan phoned again at around 01.30 and her brother told her he had tried to get out but 'couldn't because there was too much black smoke and we can't see, we can't breathe'. This went on back and forth between her brother's family, the control room and Hanan.

At 02.15, Hanan made her fourth call to her brother. Faouzia picked up. Hanan was desperate and forceful – 'Get out, get out!' Faouzia's plaintive response was, 'We are trying. We are trying'. By this stage the fire was in the kitchen of their flat.

Meanwhile, in the neighbouring flat, Ligaya had gone to bed and in all probability had turned off her mobile phone. A friend with whom she'd been out earlier in the day heard the news and quickly phoned her, to no avail.

The pathology suggests she was overcome by toxic fumes in the vicinity of her bed.

Unlike the *Marchioness* and Hillsborough, where support groups and campaigns emerged because of the disasters, at Grenfell there were associations already in existence. Long before the fire, this community had been active in attempting to create an environment, both inside and out, that was accessible and safe. They appreciated the potential, investing time and effort, pointing out shortcomings, but not finding a receptive ear. Ironically, a revealing documentary had been commissioned by the local authority, the Royal Borough of Kensington and Chelsea (RBKC), and filmed before the fire. It conveys the ambiance of the community very effectively and, at the same time, portrays the non-receptive ear! The commissioned artist and resident Constantine Gras compiled the record as the refurbishment was taking place, chronicling the joys, the trials and the tribulations of residents and their group. Movingly, some of the contributions are from people who did not survive. Especially moving is footage of irrepressible 8-year-old Medhi Wahabi*.

---

* *Grenfell: the Untold Story* (Sept 2021), produced by BBC Studios Documentary Unit for Channel 4.

The interim report into the fire stated that:

From the outset, members of the local community have said that they warned the TMO on many occasions about the hazards, both those arising from the refurbishment and more generally. There is a strong feeling among them that their voices were ignored and that if attention had been paid to them the disaster could have been avoided. There is also a strong view in many quarters that in their response to the disaster the authorities failed the community by not providing adequate support in the days immediately following the fire.[2]

The 'TMO' is the Kensington and Chelsea Tenant Management Organisation (KCTMO) – a title that belies its true nature, as it was the property management arm of RBKC. So it is not management by the tenants, but of the tenants.

These aspects were given further consideration in Phase 2 of the inquiry and will form part of the full and final report.

There were two particularly important pre-existing support groups, which complemented each other in the way they worked tirelessly towards a better environment for all, compensating for the deficiencies of authority. One was the Grenfell Action Group (GAG) and the other was the Grenfell Tower Leaseholders' Association (GTLA). A third group, named Compact, emerged in 2015, endeavouring to seal a signed agreement between the residents and the authorities for improvements to the tower, the environment and the quality of life of the residents.

GAG was formed in 2010 by Edward Daffarn and Francis O'Connor who also, in 2012, started a blog. They were committed to defending the rights of residents of the Lancaster West Estate, which included Grenfell Tower. Their targeted concern was the disingenuously termed 'regeneration' scheme by the local authority, which involved the destruction of one of the few green spaces serving this disparate social housing estate. It also involved the construction of the Kensington Academy and Leisure Centre, a prestige project which took precedence over and delayed refurbishment of Grenfell Tower, a process they described as gentrification or social cleansing. Basically, they wanted 'social justice and adequate services for our community.'

They wanted their blog to be a permanent testament to this struggle. And that is exactly what has happened. Prophetic warnings, ten in total over the previous four years. On 20 November 2016, only a matter of months before the fire, under the heading 'KCTMO – Playing with Fire', the blog post read:

It is a truly terrifying thought but the GAG firmly believe that only a catastrophic event will expose the ineptitude and incompetence of our landlord, the KCTMO, and bring an end to the dangerous living conditions and neglect of health and safety legislation that they inflict upon their tenants and leaseholders . . .

Unfortunately, the GAG has reached the conclusion that only an incident that results in loss of life of KCTMO residents will allow the external scrutiny to occur that will shine a light on the practices that characterise the malign governance of this nonfunctioning organisation . . .

It is our conviction that a serious fire in a tower block or similar high-density residential property is the most likely reason that those who wield power at the KCTMO will be found out and brought to justice! The GAG believes that the KCTMO narrowly averted a major fire disaster at Grenfell Tower in 2013 when residents experienced a period of terrifying power surges that were subsequently found to have been caused by faulty wiring.

These community-based concerns were far from isolated calls from an active corner of the estate. They were widely held, mirrored and foretold by others, none more precisely than the founder of the Grenfell Tower Leaseholders' Association, Shahid Ahmed, whom I represented – a man with a punctilious eye for detail and an assiduous desire to

meticulously expose injustice. At roughly the same time
as GAG started, he set up the GTLA as a response to an
earlier fire in the tower in 2010. As was his wont, Shah set
out his thoughts on paper, in a compelling and rigorous
manner. They need no embellishment and speak volumes.
Although they have attracted less attention than the blog,
they are unnervingly prescient.

One letter he wrote is dated 3 September 2010 (with
many more to follow) and is principally addressed to
the newly appointed CEO of the KCTMO, Robert
Black. I dubbed it the 'inferno letter' at the inquiry.
Other important players were copied in – Mr Anthony
Parkes (Director of Finance), Mr Daniel Wood (Head
of Home Ownership), Ms Sacha Jevans (Director of
Customer Service) and councillors Sir Merrick Cockell
and Judith Blakeman.

The closely argued eight-page letter flags up the main
demand and the looming threat:

> GT has been neglected for decades . . . We will argue
> that the recent fire at GT has raised so many Health
> and Safety issues with the building that it demands an
> independent investigation and inquiry into the safety of
> the building . . .
>
> We are very shocked to learn from you that you
> considered the defects in the building exposed by

the fire as a minor fault when it had potentially fatal consequences. The minor fault caused so much damage to individuals living in GT it is difficult to imagine how serious an event has to be for you to consider it a major fault.

The letter highlights a three-year fire-alarm malfunction and the absence of any evacuation procedure for the 120 families, and it poignantly foresees a core fire. Shah's wife was caught up in the 2010 fire.

As you know fire does not kill as much as the effects of smoke and to our knowledge some of the residents nearly died due to smoke inhalation and suffocation. On top of this, many residents found the whole experience traumatic and mentally damaging.

Then comes the key prediction, which would be echoed by Edward Daffarn six years later:

The staircases of the surrounding high-rise buildings are exposed to open air and natural light and so in case of a fire the smoke can easily escape. But GT with its interior staircase and malfunctioning ventilation system, there is certainly a high probability that in the event of another fire, the whole building can become an INFERNO [my emphasis]. Furthermore, should a fire occur in the staircase of GT, there will be no escape route for the residents as, and rightly so, the lift will be out of service. This raises serious health and safety issues and could trap the residents of the building in a fire with no escape.*

Shah Ahmed maintained his vigilance and his requests until shortly before the fire. One of his requests, repeated over the years, had been for a proper, comprehensive, independent safety inspection of the tower.

In the wake of the fire, fresh alignments emerged, representing the pressing and chronic needs of the survivors and the surrounding community. Two of them are Grenfell United and Justice4Grenfell. Besides the daily requirements, there are other avenues to pursue. It entails keeping a sharp eye out for the machinations of authority.

With the eyes of the world upon her, Prime Minister Theresa May had little or no option other than to establish a public judicial inquiry as quickly as possible. No waiting for thirty years before finally conceding the desirability. The Prime Minister announced the inquiry the very next

---

*   The full version of the letter can be found at inquiry pagination: TMO10037439-0001 to 0008.

day, saying, 'Right now the people want answers, and it's absolutely right, and that's why I am ordering a full public inquiry into this disaster. We need to know what happened, we need an explanation of this, we owe that to the families. To the people who have lost loved ones, friends, and the homes in which they lived.'

And, may I add, so does the UK community as a whole want answers. The issues of safety, social and racial equality, and standards in public life, all have a keen public interest for every citizen. Safe and suitable housing for all is the benchmark. This sentiment was boldly delivered by Imran Khan KC (whom I worked with on the Lawrence Inquiry) in the presence of the powers that be at the 2022 anniversary of the fire, held in Westminster Abbey. His rebuke was recorded in the *Guardian* on 14 June. A message from Grenfell to those in power: you failed us then and you are failing us now. We can't accept that.

> Of the residents of Grenfell Tower who lost their lives on the night, 85 per cent were people of colour . . . The fact is skin colour is one of the defining facts of life in the UK. If you don't feel compelled to think about it much, chances are you are white . . .
>
> The stark reality is that the race, religion, disability status and social class of the residents of the tower determined their destiny . . .

And this is where the great and the good, and those in power and in powerful institutions who have come out today to remember those who died, and comfort those who lost and suffered, must answer. Your presence is important to the bereaved, survivors and residents and wider community. But they do want to ask you this: while you are here today, where were you before the fire? Because everyone knew the fire was going to happen: it was inevitable . . .

If nothing changes, those who lost their lives will have died in vain . . .

So, when you do walk out the door today, remember this: there are no excuses for not doing something now. While your support was welcome today, if you fail to act, if you do nothing in the next 365 days before the next anniversary, you will, I am sorry to say, not be welcome then.

The familiar cry rings out yet again for truth, accountability and change. It is not a cry that echoed around the rooftops of Westminster or the Confederation of British Industry (CBI) prior to this debacle.

Within days, the penny dropped. The spectacle of the molten cladding envelope shedding itself onto the ground below, while flames burned through the window frames behind, meant this could happen again. So how many other buildings were covered in this way? Never mind the regulations, this stuff had to be removed. But nobody had a record of numbers, and nobody in the past had bothered to find out. Beyond the safety implications, the costs were astronomical. A Parliamentary Select Committee after the Garnock Court fire* in 1999 had recommended a register be compiled but, like so many recommendations, it had languished on a back-room shelf.

It has taken until 2023 to make serious inroads into the problem, with a threat to preclude manufacturers of cladding from the marketplace unless they contribute to its removal. But as a result of the broad condemnation of the cladding material – and with no action taken to remove it – many ordinary people have found themselves trapped in a bureaucratic nightmare. Unable to sell their flats, unable to even insure them, they find themselves unable to move house, unable to sleep at night without employing an expensive round-the-clock waking watch in their building. Ultimately, it was the extensive lobbying by numerous groups of residents around the country that finally made the difference. Two notable groupings in the forefront were UK Cladding Action Group (UKCAG)

---

* This fire took place on 11 June 1999 at Garnock Court, a 14-storey tower block in Irvine, Scotland, and spread via external cladding.

and the Manchester Cladiators. To provide support where needed, we formed a group of lawyers known as 'Clad-off'!

The same collective pressure on government also brought about change to the regulations themselves. The position at long last, after at least a decade of missed opportunities, is that combustible materials have finally been banned for use on the external façades of buildings. In short, the change results in banning nearly all combustible materials – including plastic, timber cladding and high-pressure laminates – on façades of residential buildings over 11m (36ft).

Without the people, this would not have been achieved so compendiously. And let us ensure in future it can be done without the deaths, as foretold, also by the people.

The economic cost is one dimension of the Grenfell story, but another – even greater – is the ongoing mental damage and stress across a wide range and a large number of people. By its nature, it is not always obvious or detectable and more often than not it is overlooked altogether.

I became acutely aware of the fallout and the chaos in the immediate aftermath of the fire as I was invited to attend and speak at a community meeting held under the Westway, which crosses this part of Notting Hill. There was an outpouring of grief and anger, of survival and resilience. Many survivors were completely bereft, their loved ones dead and their homes destroyed. There was no contingency plan in place to cope with this and no organised protective provision. Without the community and the voluntary organisations that stepped up immediately to help with food, clothes and shelter, there would have been an even worse outcome. It was reassuring to see so many familiar faces from the past gathering to lend support – one of whom was Frank Crichlow's partner Lucy*.

What tends to be overlooked in these traumatic circumstances is the far-reaching and long-lasting impact of what had been witnessed. It wasn't only those in the tower itself, but those in the immediate vicinity who could see, hear and smell the fire. And, most critically, the firefighters. Beyond them is a stunned and shocked viewing public.

As part of the preparations for evidence in the inquiry, all the lawyers were offered the opportunity to visit the tower as the families had been, if they so wished. Being carefully escorted up the 24 storeys to the roof was a mind-numbing and humbling experience.

You think you can imagine it, but nothing can prepare you for the incendiary scene where people had lived

---

* Sadly, Frank – human rights activist and founder of the Mangrove restaurant (see Chapter 3, page 45) – passed away in 2010.

their last moments. I will not describe it more as it was a deeply private and personal space, but the sight of its charred entanglements remains a vital spur for me, and for everyone in relation to what is yet to come.

A little personal reflection in relation to the devastating pain felt by loss: two years before the fire, my daughter Anna had committed suicide. At the time I was engaged in the Hillsborough Inquests, where young people – who wanted to live, unlike my daughter – had died. The families I worked with on the inquests gave me enduring support at this awful time. We had a common understanding of the heart- and soul-rending repercussions of loss.

Inspired by the support of the families, my wife-to-be Yvette Greenway and I established a mental welfare charity, SOS (Silence of Suicide). Its initial objective was simple: to enable people to off-load the stress and the pent-up guilt associated with the stigma of suicide. Not so long ago, before 1961, suicide was a crime and remains a crime if someone assists. The way we tried to help was to provide a secure place to come together as a gathering and to facilitate those who wished to unburden themselves and speak openly, often for the first time. Yvette was adept at discerning the vulnerable and facilitating their story by reassurance and encouragement. Not an unprecedented method, but one not hitherto applied to this field and therefore requiring consummate sensitivity.

We went all over the UK to very different situations, communities and institutions where we introduced this idea with very positive feedback, which was usually expressed in terms of a feeling – of being 'liberated'. Gradually the scope widened to embrace mental welfare or wellbeing generally.

After the Grenfell fire, we decided to assemble a regular series of these gatherings for anyone in the Grenfell community who might find them useful. The local church had opened a community relief, response and evacuation centre at 3am on the night. In the weeks that followed, we hosted two-hour sessions to enable personal accounts.

The first took place on Saturday 15 July at the nearby Harrow Club, in collaboration with Justice4Grenfell, other voluntary groups and the residents themselves. It was entitled 'A Safe Place to Talk'.

We had visited several times before to lay the groundwork for a highly sensitive exercise at an extremely distressing time. Our object was to allow people to speak and feel they are being heard, they are being understood and they are being taken seriously. Doing this collectively provides reassurance and prevents isolation.

For obvious reasons, individual experiences of the night and their impact are a confidence between those who came, which is part of the object. But exacerbating the horror of individual accounts was the repeated connection made by residents about how they had been treated as 'second-class citizens'. The mixed emotions, the grief, the pain and the anger were palpable and combined to foster a surge of resistance and a revival of spirit. These catalysts remain to this day very much the forces that fuel the drive for truth, accountability and change, and will not be allayed by anything less.

Thereafter, we met in the Notting Hill Methodist Church, thanks to the newly arrived minister, the Reverend Dr Mike Long. The church also became the starting point for the poignant commemorative silent march each year, which forever marks the depth and breadth of solidarity from all quarters. We learned first-hand of the suffering, and equally the spirit of revival.

In June 2022, the NHS Grenfell Health and Wellbeing Service revealed there had been 6,247 referrals, of which 1,476 were children. While these post-fire welfare services are more than welcome, in the aftermath at the time, mental wellbeing did not feature and was not a priority in official thinking.

In his closing statement to the inquiry in November 2022, Richard Millett KC concluded, 'Each and every one of the deaths that occurred in Grenfell Tower on the 14 June 2017 was avoidable'.

This is nowhere near the end. Truths have been uncovered, but there has yet to be accountability before there can be justice. You can be sure there will be no resting by the families until that has been reached.

Chapter 11
'It is Both a Dignity and a Difficulty'

The title of this chapter comes from the opening of a poem by Pádraig Ó Tuama, reflecting on the tensions of life in the North of Ireland in the 1970s and 1980s. A few lines later he poses the question:

> What about those present
> Whose past was blasted
> Far beyond their
> Future?

By 'those present' he means those left behind, who have suffered terrible personal loss. This chapter is about how those people have maintained a dignified and irrepressible mission to ensure the past is redressed to pave the way to a just future.

I have been a regular visitor to Ireland during the last half century, mostly for work. I have been repeatedly drawn by the inimitable sense of history, humour and hospitality, and ultimately got married in Belfast in 2019. I am acutely aware of where lines have been drawn, and how deep they penetrate. Yet still, it energises and engages.

The 'Troubles' is a somewhat disingenuous term for the thirty-year period of Irish history that started with a civil rights march in October 1968 and ended with the Good Friday Agreement (GFA) in 1998. The term relates to the violent relationship between sections of pro-British Protestants and the Catholic population in the North, during which time there were thousands of killings and serious injuries. It encompassed deep divisions along religious, ethnic and political lines. Pro-British Protestants were often referred to as Unionists or Loyalists. The Catholic population was not homogeneous – some were Republican, some were Nationalist, some were in favour of a United Ireland. There would be obvious overlaps but they are not synonymous terms. For example, you might be a Catholic Republican who does not accept the monarch as head of state but nevertheless has no wish to be united with Eire in the South.

The Peace Process in Northern Ireland resulted in the Good Friday Agreement in 1998, which ended the violence. Whatever its shortcomings, it remains a remarkable achievement and act of faith. It has provided a new lease of life to vibrant communities. At its core, the precondition upon which it was forged is the rule of law, not the force of the bullet. It provides the seeds of an answer to Pádraig's question on page 185, about the plight of those present.

The basis for the rule of law must be truth, followed by accountability, which constitutes justice. There can be no peace without justice. The alternative is bitter retribution and the politics of fear. That is why an integral part of the law envisaged by the agreement was the incorporation of the European Convention on Human Rights into domestic Northern Irish law, the same year as it was into UK domestic law.

Peace agreements throughout the world commonly contain provisions to deal with the legacy of past conflict. Under the broad description of transitional justice, the mechanisms aim to balance truth with accountability and, as in South Africa, an element of reconciliation. There is rarely some kind of total amnesty which grants unconditional immunity. Archbishop Desmond Tutu oversaw the Truth and Reconciliation Commission in South Africa, where a form of immunity was afforded only on very strict conditions which required a full and honest confession to wrongdoing. Without it, the perpetrator would be liable to prosecution.

I had the privilege of meeting the 'Arch' (as he wished to be called) when I was a judge on the Russell Tribunal on Palestine, sitting in Cape Town. The success and anguish of South Africa's reconciliation process is poignantly captured through the eyes of four mothers in a documentary film depicting four case studies, entitled *Long Night's Journey into Day* (2000).

The Arch visited Ireland on many occasions, including in 1998, and our discussions revolved around his attempts to initiate a Commission model in the North. I also discussed the same proposal with Mo Mowlem when she was Secretary of State for Northern Ireland in the Blair government. It was not thought to be feasible when there was effectively no change of regime.

The GFA therefore deferred legacy issues and there were no express provisions dealing with them. Related to the conflict between 1968 and 1998, there had been somewhere in the region of 3,720 deaths and 47,541 injuries. It is understandable, but regrettable, that this opportunity to construct a lasting framework for truth and accountability was regarded as a bridge too far by the politicians.

Meanwhile, back on the ground, the people most affected – which means pretty well the whole civil community in the North – had already attempted to fill the gap left by the authorities. In 1991 I chaired a People's Inquiry in Cullyhanna into the alleged 'shoot to kill' policy by the British Army (discussed in the next chapter).

In the same year, a second inquiry was sought by the families of 13 unarmed citizens killed by British soldiers in Derry on 30 January 1972 during a Northern Ireland Civil Rights Association protest march. This event has come to be known as Bloody Sunday and as well as the 13 killed on the day, 17 others were injured and a further victim died later. Those families approached British Irish Rights Watch (BIRW)*, an independent, non-governmental organisation established to monitor the violations of civil rights in the North. Collusion between the authorities and the paramilitary groups was high on the agenda. There was a particular concern for the vulnerability of lawyers. Two lawyers whom I knew well had been murdered at their homes by paramilitaries; they were Pat Finucane and Rosemary Nelson.

I had taken a very active interest in the formation of BIRW and had become a patron, assisting its tireless Director, Jane Winter, with numerous enquiries and research. It was well recognised that the first, almost immediate inquiry into Bloody Sunday – by the then Lord

---

*   Now Rights and Security International.

Chief Justice, Lord Widgery – was a whitewash and that there had been no accountability for the deaths.

The reason why all this loomed large on my radar was the quite appalling discrimination that had been suffered by the Catholic and Nationalist population in the North. It had all the trappings of colonial rule, way beyond the immediate exigencies of internment without trial. I had been initiated in the 1970s by two sisters I represented early in my career at the Bar, Dolours and Marian Price. They and others were charged and convicted of a series of bombings in London, one of which – outside the Old Bailey – blew off the roof of the first decent car I ever had and caused the library window to crash over the desk where I was sitting at lunchtime. Fortunately, no one was killed . . . a warning had been given. (Meanwhile, back at the ranch, my mother Mrs Marjorie Mansfield was becoming increasingly bewildered and bemused at my early career trajectory, wondering what on earth I was doing.)

In the lead-up to the trial in Winchester, I spent many hours in conference at the prison, listening and absorbing the sisters' life story. I was not that much older than them and kept pondering how an accident of birth was all that separated our worlds. The daily injustice and discrimination for the Catholic and Nationalist community was intolerable. It percolated through every avenue of their lives – inequalities in electoral rights, housing, employment, education, benefits, transport and communication – particularly in Derry, which was the second-largest city in the North but contained some of the poorest areas and, despite a Catholic majority, was governed by a Unionist cabal. Attempts to rectify this by recourse to the civil rights agenda were regarded as a front for terrorism and were put down by force. Public demonstrations were banned.

There was a further dimension for some Nationalists. They felt the only natural and satisfactory solution was political – a United Irish state – but this was bitterly opposed by the Unionists.

This was the background for the civil rights march and demonstration on 30 January 1972, six months after the introduction of internment without trial*. A large and peaceful crowd of around 15,000 assembled in the Creggan district of Derry. The Northern Ireland Civil Rights Association had planned they would end up at a meeting, to be addressed by well-known figures of the day –Ivan Cooper, Bernadette Devlin MP and Lord

---

* Internment without trial was deployed by the Unionist government in August 1971, allowing the authorities to confine those considered to be a risk. See Chapter 12, page 203, for more explanation.

Fenner Brockway. The route was heavily barricaded to contain the march within the Catholic areas and out of the city centre.

There came a point when the main march divided, with some heading to Free Derry Corner, leaving others to confront the barricades. Free Derry had become a symbol of civilian resistance and an ongoing thorn in the side of British rule. It was characterised as the Bogside 'no go' zone. Once the confrontation at the barricades began, elements of the British Army – who had been deployed at the march to implement a last-ditch attempt to round up so-called subversives – were sent in to execute a scoop-up arrest operation. The Paras (the Parachute Regiment) took the opportunity to shoot first and ask questions afterwards. They lost control and killed innocent citizens.

Leo Young, brother of John Young who died on the day, recalled:

'We were there. We saw what happened, but nobody wanted to know – or ever asked. My mother warned me to look after our John – he was only 17 and too young to go on marches. I said he'd be fine with his friends. He took shelter at the rubble barricade. They shot him in the face.

'I'd been arrested by the British army and taken away while trying to get someone else to hospital. The boy we were helping died. The next day, back at Strand

Road police barracks, a big detective came into the room asking if I was "Young". I said I was.

'Staring at me, he asked how many brothers I had. "Two," I replied. "You've only one now," he said. That's how I found out John was dead. When I saw the crowds outside our house, I knew he was telling the truth.'

On the corner of the Rossville Flats, Barney McGuigan stood near a telephone box with other civilians sheltering from military fire. He was 41, a highly respected married man with six children. A witness standing nearby recounted what happened in a statement I would later read to the inquiry:

'He was one of the men huddled at the wall near me. He was a community man and generally looked up to. After a short time, although I do not know how long, Mr McGuigan said that he could not stand the sound of the man calling [for help] any longer and that if he went out waving a white hanky, they would not shoot at him. We tried to dissuade him from going out. We told him they would shoot him. However, he was brave and he stepped away from us holding the white hanky in his hand. Although I cannot be certain, I think he held it in his left hand. He walked out slowly sideways in an arc towards where we thought the sound was coming from.

'He stepped out about ten to twelve feet away from us. All the time he was walking I could see the left-hand side of his face. We were calling to him all the time to come back. He kept looking back at us.'

The witness then described the terrible injury caused by a single bullet entering the back of Barney McGuigan's head and exiting through an eye. He was not only the oldest, but also the last to be shot dead on Bloody Sunday. The sounds he had heard were coming from Patrick Doherty, another father of six who was fatally wounded. In trying to help an injured man while waving the internationally recognised symbol of assistance and not hostility, Barney was doing no more than two priests caught up in similar circumstances – one on this day who survived, and one in Ballymurphy who did not (see Chapter 12, page 205).

When this witness account and those of others were put by me to the suspected perpetrator known as Soldier F at the inquiry, he finally accepted responsibility. At that moment in the Central Hall, Westminster, Barney's widow Bridie, after waiting for decades, collapsed.

After the Widgery whitewash, the families of the victims were unswerving in their absolute dedication to removing the stain on the characters of the deceased as 'terrorists' and to bring the authorities to book. They were supported by their community in this strenuous endeavour and by the outstanding efforts of local author and broadcaster Don Mullan, who assiduously researched material to counter the superficial account propounded by Widgery. The principal source was the civilian eyewitnesses who had been ignored, even though many had provided accounts at the time. Mullan published his work in a book, *Eyewitness Bloody Sunday* (1997), which became the primary catalyst for the family campaign and a dossier they submitted to the government that year.

There is now a fine memorial in the form of the Museum of Free Derry, standing in Glenfada Park, central to the killing of five and the wounding of four of the civilians. On a visit recently, they kindly gave me a photographic account of Bloody Sunday, ending with the words 'a campaign that changed the course of history'. The power in the people, dare I say?

Prime Minister Tony Blair announced the second inquiry in a statement to the House of Commons on 29 January 1998. He concluded, 'Madam Speaker, members of the families of the victims, like the HM [Honourable Member] for Foyle, have conducted a long campaign to this end. I have heard some of their remarks over recent years and have been struck by their dignity. Most do not want recrimination. They do not want revenge. But they do want the truth. I believe it is in the interests of everyone that the truth is established, and told. It is also the way forward to the necessary reconciliation which will be such an important part of building a secure future for the people of Northern Ireland. I ask all sides of the House to support our proposal for this Inquiry.'

This was barely three months before the Good Friday Agreement was signed on 10 April. In a sense, the inquiry chaired by Lord Saville was very much a vital part of the peace process, in that it was performing the role of a Truth and Reconciliation Commission, if not by name, certainly in unspoken practice. This crucial aspect is often overlooked by those who complained about its length (it was gathering evidence from 1999 to 2004). It was at the time the longest proceedings in Anglo-Irish legal history. Its place in the making of a new era is indisputable and the fallout is still being felt about the question of prosecutions.

Over the years between 1998 and 2010, when the report was finally published, the inquiry held its hearings mainly at the Guildhall in the centre of Derry, and in London at the Methodist Central Hall (again!). It was split because anonymised military witnesses refused to give evidence in Derry for security reasons. The chair, Lord Saville, assisted by two other panel members, decided on the evidence presented by counsel to the inquiry. It traversed a broad spectrum of events – political, socioeconomic, military and paramilitary and policing – all of which were absolutely central to its purposes in the context of a peace process. The killings took place over a few minutes but the backcloth was enormous. These were momentous events that could not be glossed over for a second time or treated as some kind of isolated aberration. A key feature here, as it was in other inquiries, was the question of mindset, of decision-making culture, of prejudiced presumptions. The highest echelons of Anglo-Irish governance had been infected.

When the report was finally published on 15 June 2010, amidst anxious anticipation, like Hillsborough it was organised with great care to prevent premature leaks. The Guildhall, Derry was to be the place of publication and is reminiscent of the Victorian Gothic buildings that pepper the areas of London where I had lived. Constrained grandeur, nothing too extravagant (except, unlike other buildings of its ilk, it contained a very imposing organ).

The families were given a limited preview before a public announcement by the PM at lunchtime. Space was limited, so not the whole of each family could be admitted for the preview. The others gradually filled the square outside to capacity. The square was set against the 17th-century Derry city walls, built originally to defend English settlers. The ramparts provided an ideal film, television and radio gantry. I think we were in a room up at one end of the Guildhall, behind the organ, with latticed windows which did not permit a view of the square outside.

Each team was given an 11-volume copy of the report and roughly three hours to read it. The rapid absorption of 11 volumes clearly had to be divided up. There could be a myriad of different findings for different clients, so they could not all be in the same room listening to the sighs and grunts of the lawyers performing a speed read. We had just three hours to get it right. Our team comprised three diligent Derry solicitors – Des, Paddy and Greg – and three barristers – me, John and Kieran. That wasn't enough to cover all the volumes, let alone read them in depth – let alone provide considered advice with analysis and potential ramifications. However, the families were far less panic stricken than we were!

As it happened, there was a deal of common ground and the main conclusions were strikingly damning. As soon as this became clear, cheers went up in distant parts of the building in the hope this might percolate into the streets outside and inform the crowds. But then some acrobatic fanatic (excuse the language) in our room managed to elevate himself into a position whereby he was able to prise open a long casement window, quite unused to such treatment, and stick his hand through the slim gap with a thumbs up. That set the whole square off.

When the newly elected Prime Minister David Cameron rose to speak, we were more than ready. It was a statesman-like delivery, as demanded by the gravity of the occasion. What he reported was breathtaking. We understood later, from those who had seen the speech notes, that the handwritten annotations indicated that the Prime Minister had taken a personal interest in ensuring that the wording conveyed a precise picture.

Within a minute of commencing, he said, 'Lord Saville concludes that the soldiers of Support Company who went into the Bogside did so as a result of an order which should not have been given by their Commander . . . He finds that none of the casualties shot by the soldiers of Support Company was armed with a firearm . . . He also finds that the Support Company reacted by losing their self-control, forgetting or ignoring their instructions and training, and with a serious widespread loss of fire discipline . . . He finds that despite the contrary evidence given by the soldiers, none of them fired in response to attacks or threatened attacks by nail or petrol bombers . . . And he finds that many of the soldiers, and I quote, 'knowingly put forward false accounts to seek to justify their firing' . . . Crucially, that, and I quote, 'none of the casualties was posing a threat of causing death or serious injury, or indeed was doing anything else that could on any view justify the shooting . . .'

'But what happened should never ever have happened. The families of those who died should not have had to live with the pain and hurt of that day and with a lifetime of loss . . . I would also like to acknowledge the grief of the families of those killed. They have pursued their long campaign over the last 38 years with great patience . . .

'Mr Speaker, this report and the inquiry itself demonstrate how a state should hold itself to account and how we should be determined at all times, no matter how difficult, to judge ourselves against the highest standards . . . Openness and frankness about the past, however painful, do not make us weaker, they make us stronger.'

These pertinent sentiments apply to hundreds of other similar instances which are yet to be acknowledged in the same manner, now referred to as the 'legacy cases'. And the fallout from Bloody Sunday itself is still being pursued patiently and persistently.

We can distil three major features Bloody Sunday had in common with the *Marchioness*, Hillsborough and Grenfell:

1. It's not about the nature of the incident, but rather the nature of the governance and the culture it cultivates.
2. It's not governance that recognises the malfeasance and forces change, but the persistence of the people.

3. The malfeasance identified does not arise out of the blue, like some weird aberration that has taken everyone by surprise.

Inquiries have a habit of exposing the attitudes and actions that lead to these events as part of a pattern of underlying denial and dishonesty. Using Bloody Sunday as an example, you don't all suddenly go berserk on your own soil at the same time, all managing to inadvertently kill the wrong people and then all coming up with the same story that you thought the dead victims were gunmen. The somewhat dramatic shift by the army at the inquiry – from their original position that the dead were terrorists – left both versions of their story lacking any credibility. The big unanswered question second time around was that if all the victims were mistakenly killed, where are all the gunmen they specifically identified and claimed they'd killed first time round?

The truth was that this didn't happen out of the blue. Many readers in Ireland will know about this, but in Britain there is less awareness – there had already been another Bloody Sunday in Ballymurphy just five months before. A similarly unanswerable conundrum arose in the Ballymurphy inquests as those for Bloody Sunday. In both instances, of course, the answer lies in fundamental dishonesty.

Chapter 12
The Ballymurphy Massacre

A year before Bloody Sunday, at the commencement of the desperate policy of internment in August 1971, the same British Army regiment – the Paras – was meting out the same treatment, only in Ballymurphy not Derry. It has been described as Belfast's Bloody Sunday.

Internment, or the confinement of those considered to be hostile or to pose a threat, has a long and inglorious history. It happened in both world wars to those categorised as 'enemy aliens'. It happened during the colonial exploits of the major European nations when the term 'internment' became synonymous with concentration. You are detained en masse, not because of any proven criminal offence, but purely on account of your beliefs, your nationality, your associations. It's no surprise it was called 'internment without trial'.

A decision to use this tactic was taken at the highest level by the Unionist Prime Minister of Northern Ireland Brian Faulkner and the British Home Secretary Reginald

Maudling. It was aimed at the Catholic and Republican communities – they were all tarred with the terrorist brush. No Unionist, nor Loyalist, nor Protestant communities were targeted, let alone their allied paramilitary groupings like the Ulster Defence Association and the Ulster Volunteer Force.

To enforce internment, the British Army was deployed as back-up to the civilian Royal Ulster Constabulary. It began in the early hours of 9 August 1971, when 340 people were detained, based on highly dubious and outdated intelligence and erroneous information. The force used was indiscriminate. The killings took place over the course of three days in five separate but proximate locations in Ballymurphy. Ten civilians died at the time and one later. The damage done was irredeemable. Later, the operation would be described as the best recruiting sergeant the IRA had ever had.

To accommodate the numbers, special detention facilities were developed, like the infamous blocks at Long Kesh (the Maze). Shocking 'interrogation in depth' methods were employed, which included hooding. For innocent citizens caught up in the middle of this onslaught, it takes a great deal of inner strength and commitment to rise above this level of physical and psychological oppression.

Once more, this provides a striking example and testament to the endurance of truth over falsehood – in this case fifty years, from 1971 to 2021. In this age of fake news, it makes a refreshing change for truth to survive and triumph so conclusively. It is an outstanding achievement by the families and their community who nurtured it steadfastly. From day one, they never took their eyes off the ball – the simple truth was that not one of the deceased was a gunman or a gunwoman.

Prima facie – as lawyers are prone to drone, which means 'on the face of it' – you could tell immediately from at least two of the victims that this was a massacre.

The first was a highly respected and well-known local priest, Father Hugh Mullan. He was crawling across waste ground outside his house to care for and anoint a neighbour, Bobby Clarke, who had been shot in the back while protecting children, but ultimately survived. Not that the firer cared. There was a general belief by the military that anything that moved in a predominately Catholic area must be a Nationalist, and therefore a Republican who was either a member, or a fellow traveller, of the IRA and, consequently, was fair game. An elision and culture fostered by those in authority. Father Mullan had telephoned the nearby Henry Taggart Army Base to let them know what he was about to do and brandished a white garment, lest there be any doubt. He was shot from behind by two or three high-velocity rounds and was assessed by the pathology to have been lying down, kneeling or crouching at the moment of impact.

A second victim was a 44-year-old mother-of-eight, Joan Connolly, who had momentarily and mistakenly thought – as she provided cups of tea to British troops – that they were coming to the rescue of a besieged community. On that night she had been worried about the safety of her children and had gone to look for her daughter Briege. On her way home, she crossed the open ground called the Manse, which was directly in front of the army base.

Soldiers at the base opened fire. Joan went to help a young man, Noel Phillips. As she did so, near the gable end of a house at the edge of the Manse and in view of an eyewitness, she was blasted. A high-velocity bullet scorched through her left eye and took off half her face. She was shot a further three times and left unattended, bleeding to death.

Soldiers returned days later to taunt the family by singing, 'Where's your mama gone?'

The story peddled by the authorities was unnervingly like Bloody Sunday. The deceased had been posing a threat, carrying weapons and – in one incident – the army had come under fire from at least twenty IRA gunmen in a battle lasting three hours.

Once victims' families are tarred with this brush, it is a long hard struggle to remove the stain and stigma. But you cannot turn away. There can be no rest until the slate is clean, until authority has been made to face the truth for the benefit of all.

The hurdles were huge.

The initial investigation was a shocking travesty. A deal had been set up between the army and the police that any preliminary investigation and taking of statements would not be done by the police. Instead it would be kept in-house and be conducted by the Royal Military Police (RMP). The interviews with soldiers would not be under caution, but would be ordinary witness statements for administrative purposes. Provided no offence was disclosed, that was the end of it. This was an easy ride for soldiers.

If they killed someone, they could just say it was self-defence, which would not disclose an offence requiring investigation. It was made even easier by another ruse. To avoid any possibility of criminal liability for individual soldiers, it would be argued that the statements had been obtained by compulsion – namely superior orders. In other words, they would be afforded a form of immunity. This so-called protocol is presently creating havoc with potential prosecutions, despite strong judicial disapproval of these original policy agreements.

Alongside all these impediments to justice, there was no scientific examination of the scenes, no ballistic analysis, no witness gathering. The unofficial line was basically: What do you expect? We are fighting an undeclared war.

The inquest hearings were inconclusive and customarily returned formal open verdicts. No soldiers gave live evidence – their statements were merely read under cyphers, which meant they couldn't be identified because all the lists showing who was Soldier A, B, C or Z were mysteriously mislaid! The job of tracking who they were was laborious and depended on the Ministry of Defence using other means.

Undeterred by all this obfuscation and obstruction, the families still fought on. They were ably supported throughout by a solicitor who had grown up in Belfast, who recognised the pressures facing all citizens and had established a community-based human rights law firm – Pádraig Ó Muirigh. Their application for fresh inquests was granted in 2011*.

The inquests opened in 2018 before the Right Honourable Mrs Justice Siobhan Keegan (who would subsequently become the first Lady Chief Justice of Northern Ireland). For me, being back in Belfast was like returning to a second

---

* A documentary feature film by Callum Macrae, *The Ballymurphy Precedent* (2018), is a compelling record of all these events.

home. There was warmth and familiarity round every corner. It was the prospect of examining General Sir Mike Jackson, former Chief of Staff and Head of the British Army, for a second time that I was particularly looking forward to. The first time I'd examined him was at the Bloody Sunday Inquiry, when he had had difficulty explaining a 'shot list' of firers, in his handwriting, that he had drawn up, which did not fit the topography, let alone the location of where bodies were found. His list was at the heart of the government's public justification of the shootings.

In Ballymurphy, he was the Adjutant and Press Officer for 1 PARA (the First Battalion, Parachute Regiment). This time his difficulty was a headline in the *Belfast Telegraph* which was derived from his report that 'We killed two of them [gunmen] and recovered their bodies'. This was meant to refer to John Laverty and Joe Corr. I represented one of these two families.

According to Mrs Justice Siobhan Keegan, however, both men were unarmed, there 'was no evidence of paramilitary trappings associated with the deceased' and the shooting was not justified. She went on to make express reference to the 'gunmen' description by saying, 'It had been wrong to describe the two men as gunmen at the time and that rumour should be dispelled.'

Her full findings in 2021 were a model of clarity and reasoning.

It was unequivocally a complete exoneration, a vindication for the long-suffering families and their community, for all the victims. None of them was armed or presented a threat to the army. Nine out of the ten who died at the time were shot by the army. It was not possible to determine the fate of the tenth.

There was no justification for the fatal shots by the army. The treatment of Joan Connolly was described as 'basic inhumanity'. Her final words expressed 'the hope that some peace may be achieved now that the findings of the inquest have been delivered.'

No peace without justice, which is vital for the North. Yet ultimately, no accountability by those in power, nor those who pulled the trigger.

But despite the judgement of the inquiry, this chapter documenting the Ballymurphy story sadly does not end there. There are times when the people in power just can't help their instincts. They cling on to whatever vestiges of superiority they feel have survived. To accept defeat, even fifty years after the event, is inconceivable.

In 2021, minutes before the Northern Ireland Secretary Brandon Lewis stood to announce an apology in Parliament in relation to Ballymurphy, the families received a letter from Prime Minister Boris Johnson.

After fifty years of sweat, blood and tears from the families, it was a perfunctory four paragraphs, given as if he were going through the motions, following a template, no more – an apology for the grief and an acceptance of the coroner's findings. John Teggart, whose father Daniel was unlawfully killed, said the tone and the timing were unacceptable.

Of particular interest was paragraph 3, which read:

The duty of the State is to hold itself to the highest standard and that requires us to recognise the hurt and agony caused where we fall short of those standards. For what happened on those terrible few days in Ballymurphy, and for what the families have gone through since you began your brave and dignified campaign almost five decades ago, I am truly sorry.

Not a word about the highest standards implicit in Article 2 of the European Convention (the right to life) requiring accountability. Not a word about the absence of those rights to life from the start for these killings. This was all part of the deep-seated and long-standing belief in some quarters of the Conservative Party that there should be immunity for troops engaged in this way, supported by veterans' organisations who actively seek to dissuade soldiers from coming forward to give evidence.

In 2005, there had been an attempt to fill the gap left by the GFA and combine the investigation of unsolved killings (of which there are approximately a breathtaking 3,000) with a form of closure and reconciliation for the families who would be at the heart of the process.

It was established by the then Chief Constable of the Police Service of Northern Ireland (PSNI) Sir Hugh Orde. The unit, entitled Historical Enquiries Team (HET), had two branches – review and investigation. It was disbanded in 2014 amid claims that its investigative standards were less than robust and consistent, and claims of budgetary reconfiguration.

At that point, the British and Irish governments and four out of the five main parties – after several attempts – finally signed up to the Stormont House Agreement. This proposed an independent historical investigations unit to examine outstanding cases and to acquire confidential information about the deaths for the benefit of relatives. This has been termed the 'right of recountability' in academic circles. The mechanisms for this were prepared, but shortly thereafter Mr Johnson in his usual cavalier manner ditched the agreement in favour of an amnesty for Troubles-related crimes, driven by a cabal of his party who wished to protect the military. His replacement scheme, the Northern Ireland Troubles (Legacy and Reconciliation) Bill, is not only a misnomer but also a direct repudiation of the justice so long delayed. It seeks to put an end to all Troubles-related litigation – criminal, civil and coronial – and it fundamentally undermines the GFA as well as our ECHR obligations. It is opposed by substantial sectors of the people – all the political parties in the North, the Council of Europe (not to be confused with the European Union), the UN Rapporteur, the Northern Ireland Human Rights Commission, Liberty and the Irish Government.

Currently a cutoff date for the end of any remaining litigation has been set for 1 May 2024, which has cast a shadow and a blight over the legacy work.

That is why we repeat, emphatically: please can it not be the people in power?

Chapter 13
Taking the Law into Your Own Hands

Without a fanfare of publicity, a movement has been developing imperceptibly alongside the gradual awakening that has occurred in the individual miscarriages of justice cases and the various movements allied to cases involving race, feminism, peace, social justice and safety. It derives from the inner force we all possess, described by the philosopher Bertrand Russell as 'conscience' – an unequivocal feeling for fairness and justice.

If that feeling is ignored, frustrated, oppressed or suppressed, the people have begun to realise that they can take it upon themselves to rectify the situation, not just with political remedies but also with quasi-judicial processes. At a political and global level, there have been distinct occasions over the last fifty years when citizens whose rights have been denied have taken to the streets in various pro-democracy movements. They have toppled regimes, brought down walls and shaken foundations.

Then there are 'democratic' countries where there is a significant democratic deficit, where the voice of the population is not proportionately or adequately represented, nor is it taken seriously.

This is the unmistakable view of many towards the British Parliamentary system.

An international political initiative in 2011 – the Occupy movement – successfully and peacefully drew attention to the impact of social and economic inequality by occupying public spaces near symbolic institutions around the world. A memorable one in London took place on the steps of St Paul's Cathedral, on the edge of the City, or banking sector. Besides the physical space they occupied, they made good use of social media to create the seeds of collective direct democracy by engaging in deliberation and discussion, some of which I joined as my chambers were nearby. The response of authority was to threaten forceful eviction, not dialogue. The cathedral authorities permitted police intervention, a prospect that caused the Canon Chancellor of St Paul's, Giles Fraser, to resign.

In tandem with the political momentum motivated by a growing democratic deficit, bordering on bankruptcy, an alternative quasi-judicial process has emerged – Citizens' Assemblies, born out of the efforts of civil society. The result has been the formation of civil associations across national divides, providing an inclusive and diverse forum on issues of general import. An example goes under the title 'Another Europe is Possible', which has recently been tackling social justice, threats to human rights, refugees and the war in Ukraine. Another is Compass – together for a good society. This has become known as 'deliberative democracy'.

At a more local level, but in a less demonstrative manner, the same motivation has revolved around forms of injustice that are not being addressed by the state. In the past, this has mostly arisen as a 'reaction' to initiatives taken by the state which need to be countered. Where, however, the state has failed to act – especially in relation to its human rights obligations – citizens have turned to other ways of challenging the failures: a 'proactive' approach. Distinct from the Assemblies, these take the form of Citizens' Tribunals or People's Commissions of Inquiry. While they don't have legal powers of compulsion or discovery, nor public funding like judicial inquiries (hence 'quasi'), they endeavour to apply the judicial principles of due process and fairness.

A former and ambitious incarnation of this concept was conceived and convened by the eminent British philosopher and Nobel Prize-winner Bertrand Russell. He saw it as a tribunal of conscience, the 'conscience of mankind', which would examine how the norms, tenets and obligations of international law had been violated and had not been pursued by the organs of international governance.

Bertrand Russell's famous exhortation at the opening of the International War Crimes Tribunal in 1966 was, 'May this tribunal prevent the crime of silence'. His focus was the controversial Vietnam War and whether the US government had committed acts of aggression. He gathered in 1966–67 a bevy of international intellectual celebrities, which endowed the project with standing and profile. Jean-Paul Sartre, renowned French existentialist philosopher, chaired it, and other distinguished figures – the Italian jurist Lelio Basso and the prominent writer James Baldwin – joined the panel. Eighteen countries participated. Its final report played a significant part in mobilising global opinion against the war.

Since then, there has been a series of less publicised 'Russell' tribunals in relation to other theatres of oppression and war, such as Latin America and the Iraq War.

In March 2009, the Bertrand Russell Peace Foundation inaugurated one on the Israeli-Palestine conflict. I had the honour of being asked to sit on the panel of international judges. The tribunal began in Barcelona and finished in New York with an opportunity to address a committee of the United Nations General Assembly (UNGA). There were numerous well-documented Israeli government transgressions, some recorded by the International Court of Justice (2004), concerning the erection of a wall of separation and the illegal occupation of Palestinian land. I have visited Palestine myself and seen conditions on the ground, which are abhorrent.

The undoubted figurehead was the intellectual goliath to whom I have dedicated this book – Stéphane Hessel. An escapee from two Nazi concentration death camps, a member of the French Resistance, a key contributor to the draft Universal Declaration of Human Rights in 1948 and, thereafter, a prominent French diplomat at the UN, Stéphane Hessel was a passionate advocate of the tribunal and its principles. He attended every session. From our regular conversations, I appreciated that there was no predicament that could not be countered or addressed by the effective deployment of basic human rights law.

It was Stéphane's pamphlet or tract entitled *Indignez-vous!*, published in 2010, that captured the imagination and mood globally. He explained it was his final cri de coeur, at the age of 93, for people to be 'outraged' at the inequalities that surround us. It became the inspiration for the Indignados protests in Madrid, the Arab Spring as a whole, the Occupy Wall Street movement – and this book!

His message can be conveyed in a brief aphorism: *Be indignant, not indifferent.* At the beginning of his autobiography, *The Power of Indignation*, he takes this message further by saying:

Outrage must find its true path and result in actual engagement. For were outrage to remain in this formless state of antagonism and were it to wither and turn to anger, nothing would come of it but some gnashing of teeth. Nevertheless, determining what deserves our outrage is the first skill I owe myself to teach those who are going to be protesting this new world and the grave dangers we face. It all boils down to having a conscience.

The conclusion of the Israeli-Palestine Tribunal was that the regime imposed on Palestinians amounted to apartheid, and that action should be taken by the UN to bring this to an end. We realised this was hindered by the perennial problem of a UN Security Council (UNSC) forever split between the US and Russia, with the UK abstaining whenever it could. This renders initiating an International Criminal Court (ICC) prosecution virtually impossible. We also argued that the basis of the UNSC must be radically changed to overcome the impasse, by enlarging the composition and by abolishing the veto.

A year or so later I was invited to participate in another Russell-style People's Tribunal.

Terrible atrocities had been committed by the regime of the ayatollahs in Iran in the 1980s and constituted crimes against humanity. There had been no justice for the families, friends and relatives of the victims. Inspired by a group of women, the Mothers of Khavaran, the relatives took justice into their own hands and established a sophisticated and effective tribunal, supported by a number of human rights organisations.

It was divided into two stages. The first was a Commission of Truth which sat in London and was hosted by Amnesty International. Its aim was to establish the facts from the testimony of survivors, human rights groups and the UN Special Rapporteur. The second stage was adjudication, sitting in the Peace Palace in The Hague, Netherlands, which houses the International Court of Justice (ICJ). The case was set out by Sir Geoffrey Nice KC, an accomplished and experienced advocate at the International Criminal Court, also situated in The Hague, assisted by a team led by Hamid Sabi. The report was a searing indictment of human rights violations and led to the establishment of a foundation to continue the tribunal's work, part of which involves monitoring the movement of Iranian suspects who could be detained by individual governments should they enter their jurisdiction[*].

★

---

[*] Sweden has already done this.

The examples above are one end of a spectrum. Although playing out at an international level, they nonetheless exemplify what is possible by collective endeavour and application at the other end. This has been gradually taking hold in the UK, where I have been involved in four Citizens' Tribunals and was the chair of a panel in each one. The first examined evidence suggesting the British Army employed a shoot-to-kill policy in Northern Ireland. It was organised by the National Congress and the Community Justice Group in Cullyhanna, County Armagh, who were shocked by the killing of Fergal Caraher and the wounding of his brother by Royal Marine Commandos in December 1990. There were three jurists from the USA, France and Germany. The inquiry was established quickly, within months of the killing. The security situation was tense. I was allocated a bodyguard in case of a stray bullet and accommodated across the border in the Republic.

The second and third were both in relation to hospital closure in London – one in Lewisham, Southeast London, and the other in Northwest London. They were commissioned by the councils of Hammersmith and Fulham, Ealing, Hounslow and Brent. Lay and professional witnesses were called in both instances and were questioned by experienced barristers. The common denominator of government policy was rigorously scrutinised in these cases, particularly the fragmentation of the NHS by the creation of an internal market and the increased use of private providers and consortia. It is still an issue today. At least for now the closures were forestalled in Lewisham and especially the Charing Cross Hospital in Hammersmith. Funding of such inquiries is extremely hard work and is a mixed basket. Crowdfunding, voluntary contributions, trade unions, civil rights groups and local authorities help to keep matters afloat.

In a sense, these inquiries were the appetisers and forerunners for what came next and what is happening now.

Covid. Worldwide, no one has gone unscathed. Public health provision has been severely tested. Whole patterns of living have altered. Attitudes and priorities have had to be adjusted.

From Covid's inception in 2019–20 until now, the big question on everyone's lips has been: how has this been allowed to happen? Essentially, it's the same question that underlies all the inquiries and inquests we have examined. How can recurrence be prevented?

The equally big question in 2020 was duration. No one, least of all government, really knew how long a pandemic of this magnitude might last. It did not take long for the people to realise that besides blatant rule-breaking by the rule-makers, there were confused and mixed messages emanating daily from the portals of Downing Street, accompanied by serious misjudgements about quarantine, types of isolation, social distancing, care homes, provision of protective equipment, mega hospitals, and the capacity of the ambulance service.

The call soon went up in 2020 for an 'inquiry', becoming louder and more incessant as the months of chaos proceeded. It was most urgent among the bereaved who had suffered the separation and the intense anguish of not being able to comfort the dying in their moment of greatest need.

This call went unheeded initially, but was subsequently rejected as being too early and distracting. Many concerned health workers, professionals, bereaved and members of the public felt strongly that lessons had to be learned immediately to alleviate the risk of repetition. They were also concerned that although the NHS still had some of the best services in the world, despite having been run down by successive governments, these services were largely being overlooked for the benefit of the private sector.

As a lawyer, and having been so intimately involved in the process over many years, I was acutely aware of the predicament. To undertake an inquiry that will attract public confidence, establish the facts, assess causation and provide sensible guidelines is unquestionably an immense task that could take years, and has done so in the past. The preparation alone can take a year or more before a word of evidence is heard in public. Finding a venue and assembling personnel is the same. The hearings, split into modules, are bound to occupy two to three years. By the time it finally reports, the urgency has disappeared, memories have faded and circumstances have changed (maybe government as well). Hence it is the fate of many a final report to languish on a distant Whitehall shelf – or, nowadays, in a digital depository – as a monument to our history.

To avoid these pitfalls, I suggest that the recent examples set by the people have much to be said in their favour and contain the seeds for a more rapid, responsive and inclusive model for future generations.

And so it was that in the winter of 2020, a group of medics and others bound together by a commitment to the NHS decided to establish a People's Covid Inquiry. Its aim was to confront the critical situation facing the public without further delay, there being no sign of Mr Johnson welcoming any form of public investigation, despite the persistent pleas from the bereaved.

Tony and Olivia O'Sullivan – who have devoted their lives to public health – ably assisted by Tom Griffiths, provided both the inspiration and the backbone for the construction and scope of this inquiry. Besides the urgent need to learn and apply lessons before it was too late, there was also a plethora of potential violations of international legal obligations which should be identified, investigated, rectified and sanctioned. A flavour of the obligations can be found in the Universal Declaration of Human Rights[3], the Charter of the UN[4], the Constitution of the World Health Organization (1946) and the World Health Assembly (1948), the International Health Regulations (2005), and the International Covenant on Economic, Social and Cultural Rights[5]. Add to this the European Convention on Human Rights and the UK Human Rights Act and you have quite a lot to be getting on with.

One of the main issues underlying this legal superstructure is preparedness and response – put more concisely, the foreseeable risk of a pandemic recurrence. This is no mean burden for citizens to bear when government is reticent and recalcitrant. It was a pretty obvious decision for Mr Johnson: don't set up an inquiry that has any chance of providing even an interim report which might uncover serious failings before the next General Election in 2024.

It took constant pressure from the bereaved, the public and, ultimately, the Archbishop of Canterbury to even obtain a public commitment to hold one. Very few details were forthcoming.

The first announcement of any importance was the identity of the chair which, intriguingly, was revealed just 14 days after we published the final report of the People's Covid Inquiry in December 2021.

A prime task for the people's inquiry had been to assemble a distinguished panel, whose credentials could in no way be undermined. Three experts willingly volunteered. Their knowledge and experience of the principles and the practice of public health are second to none.

- Professor Neena Modi (MB, ChB, MD, FRCP, FRCPCH, FFPM, FMedSci) – Professor of Neonatal Medicine at Imperial College London and President of the British Medical Association.
- Dr Tolullah Oni – Urban Epidemiology and Public Health Physician at the Medical Research Council Epidemiology Unit Cambridge, and Fellow of Wolfson College Cambridge and the African Academy of Sciences.
- Dr Jacky Davis – Consultant NHS Radiologist at the Whittington Hospital in North London, BMA Council member and a prolific writer on the plight of the NHS.

Then there was me – Chair.

The idea was to hit the ground running and tackle the main concerns as soon as possible. Because of the restrictions of Covid, it would have to be conducted remotely, in itself unique. We used an enlarged webinar, in which the main participants can see each other on screen but everyone else is an observer with the ability to contribute written questions both before and during the hearing.

We imposed target dates and time constraints on hearings and the length of oral testimony (20–30 minutes) to cover the ground. The hearings were fortnightly from 24 February to 16 June 2021, live streamed, each lasting just over two hours. It is remarkable how a time constraint focusses the mind and concentrates the argument.

This meant that there was a mountain of evidence and submissions in writing. All material was taken into account, whether oral or written, for the purposes of a preliminary and then a final report. It is now all available online.

Public judicial inquiries are customarily divided into a series of modules, separated by intervals for preparation and assimilation. It was imperative the People's Inquiry adopt a similar structure. There were eight sessions:

1. Preparedness
2. Government response
3. Public health strategy

4. Impact on population
5. Impact on frontline staff
6. Inequalities and discrimination
7. Procurement and profiteering
8. Governance

To make sense of this novel transmission format, an experienced barrister colleague kindly agreed to act as counsel to the inquiry – Lorna Hackett of Hackett and Dabbs. This has become the norm in all major inquests and inquiries over recent years. She had the responsibility for assembling the evidence, ensuring it was relevant and admissible, opening the proceedings and calling the witnesses. Where it was anticipated that criticism might be levelled at certain individuals or groups, they would be warned and invited to submit evidence of their own. Unsurprisingly, no government department or agency was willing to participate.

The witnesses who did contribute were exceptional and of the highest calibre. The full list of those giving oral testimony can be found in Appendix 2 of the report. This is a sample:

- Three representatives of Covid-19 Bereaved Families for Justice, who we felt should occupy centre stage

- Frontline workers in nursing, care, education, transport and migrant care
- Pensioners
- Representatives from the disabled community
- Sheffield Community Contact Tracers
- The leader of Hammersmith Council
- The MP for Leamington and Warwick

At its core were a large number of esteemed public health practitioners and experts. Again, here is a sample, although there were many more, as well as all the written material:

- Professor Sir David King – Chair of Independent SAGE
- Professor Michael Baker – Department of Public Health, University of Otago, New Zealand
- Professor Sir Michael Marmot – Director, UCL Institute of Health Equity
- Professor Stephen Reicher – Social Psychology, St Andrews University
- Professor Kamlesh Khunti – Primary Care, Diabetes and Vascular Medicine, University of Leicester and Chair of SAGE Ethnicity subgroup
- Dr Chidi Ejimofo – NHS Consultant in Emergency Medicine

- Professor David McCoy – Global Public Health, Institute of Population Health Sciences, Queen Mary University London
- Professor Jonathan Portes – Economics and Public Policy, King's College London
- Gabriel Scally – President of Epidemiology and Public Health Section, Royal Society of Medicine
- Dr John Lister – academic and health journalist

The findings and the recommendations of the panel were couched in different forms for ease and speed of reference – a preliminary set of observations; a sixty-page executive summary; a fuller 230-page report containing appendices and all the extensive references; and finally the whole lot, witness evidence et al, retained online!

Compendiously, the whole publication was entitled *Misconduct in Public Office – Why did so many thousands die unnecessarily?* The word 'misconduct' has a general, vernacular meaning understood by all, but it also has a legal meaning and constitutes a criminal offence. For behaviour to be categorised as misconduct in public office, it must be serious enough to amount to an abuse of the public's trust in the office holder and 'must amount to an affront to the standing of the public office held. The threshold is a high one requiring conduct so far below acceptable standards as to amount to an abuse of the public's trust in the office holder'[6]. (Anyone spring to mind? Say no more!)

The report was submitted to the Metropolitan Police on the day of publication in December 2021 but ever since it seems they have been in a spot of bother themselves and it will come as no surprise that the report seems to have suffered the same fate as much of the evidence of Partygate and other government Covid transgressions – No Further Action.

I have set out the logistics and the substance of this tribunal because, in my view, we managed to achieve inside one year the essence of what the public needed to know at that time about lessons and violations. Inevitably the same exercise, with far more resources and powers of compulsion, will take the official inquiry – once it gets down to the business of hearing the evidence in the summer of 2023 – another five or six years or more to complete, although the target is to do so by 2026.

This is not intended as any criticism of Baroness Heather Hallett, who was an accomplished High Court judge, adept at case management. That's just how the system operates: it's exponentially bigger if finer detail is required, or the attendance of the people in power – in government and in commerce – to provide a modicum of accountability.

But we would argue there is a strong case for what might be termed a permanent 'Rapid Response Public Inquiry Unit', endowed with the powers and funding of the longer-term ad hoc Judicial Inquiry. Critical and damaging situations that require urgent attention are on the increase. They present rapidly and have national and international ramifications. Dealing with them cannot be left to the whims and fancies of those in power.

Chapter 14
Unfinished Business

The dynamics of change, as I discussed at the beginning of this book, mean that movement is an integral and constant element of our lives. It is a necessary force in everyone which can be harnessed to give direction and outcome – however great the hurdles seem and however limited the available resources seem. There is therefore always more to do, another move to make.

Perhaps the biggest move of all at present concerns global warming and climate change. In large measure, the fate of the planet and the very existence of humankind are at our door.

There have been clear warnings over the last 25 years, initially denied by the equivalent of the flat-earth believers, but gradually recognised from the very dramatic extreme weather events that have beset different parts of the world – melting ice caps, rising sea levels, floods and mudslides, wildfires, drought and heatwaves.

The global rise in temperature of 1.5°C – identified by the Intergovernmental Panel on Climate Change as the rise we should not exceed – is looming, beyond which we are told the planet's ability to dissipate and soak up carbon dioxide will be substantially weakened and global warming will run out of control altogether. It is a generally accepted truth that carbon emissions and the carbon footprint must be drastically reduced now.

At the same time, international and national governance has failed to make sufficient inroads. There has been a great deal of talk and agreement, but scant results, with pledges, for example, of financial aid to the poorest and most vulnerable nations not being met.

Take COP, the Conference of the Parties set up under the auspices of the UN. The umbrella grouping was called the Framework Convention on Climate Change and the inaugural conference was in 1995 in Berlin. Since then, there have been annual meetings – number 26 being in Glasgow in 2021. Number 27 was held in Egypt, where the government seriously harassed climate change activists in order to silence them before the summit, according to Human Rights Watch.

The talking goes on and on all through the night but once the delegates depart, it's back to business as usual. In December 2022, the UK announced plans to open the first new coal mine in thirty years in Cumbria.

To accentuate the urgency, thousands of people gathered outside the palace of power where inside the delegates postured. No wonder Greta Thunberg described the Glasgow Conference as a 'Greenwash festival':

The people in power can continue to live in their bubble filled with their fantasies – like eternal growth on a finite planet, and technological solutions that will suddenly appear seemingly out of nowhere and will erase all of these crises just like that. All this while, the world is literally burning, on fire . . .

Her main point is that lowering emission levels is too little, too late. It must be halted now. According to the Office for National Statistics, three-quarters of adults asked were worried about the climate crisis. While not everyone will identify with Greta Thunberg, nor wish to become an eco-warrior, those who are worried can take various actions, which can make a real difference and influence change.

At a global level, there are several initiatives that would welcome support. I will mention one that has gathered enormous momentum over the last two decades. Although it is a law-based initiative, you don't have to be a lawyer to get involved – being a worried person is the main incentive and qualification.

In the wake of two major wars – WW2 and Vietnam – there were moves to protect the environment against some of the worst effects. In the 1970s, this resulted in an international prohibition on the use of military/hostile agents that cause widespread and long-lasting or severe damage to the environment (for example, Agent Orange).

The term 'ecocide' was employed during these discussions, as a recognised and convenient way of describing the banned activity. It soon became obvious that military use was not the only source of destruction. Industrial and commercial enterprises (such as oil extraction) can also devastate land and sea.

Momentum gathered to elevate and criminalise 'ecocide' by including it in the Code of Crimes Against the Peace and Security of Mankind being considered for the International Criminal Court (ICC). The others among the five crimes were genocide, war crimes, crimes against humanity and aggression. Three made it into the International Statute book* – of the two that didn't, one was aggression, which did not become an effective provision until 2018.

The other was 'ecocide'. There had been extensive discussion on the topic, often mired in scholastic argument about the intentional use of force, but still a proposal was

---

* The Rome Statute of the International Criminal Court 1998.

put forward to include it. Late on, it was withdrawn in mysterious circumstances. It is not difficult to discern potential reasons for the major nations in the UN to backtrack – those with vested interests in the oil and petroleum industry, and in the development of nuclear power in all its forms, were concerned they might end up in the dock themselves.

This was a critical setback. But the baton was immediately picked up by citizens' initiatives, especially among the smaller, vulnerable island nations.

Here in the UK, it was at this stage I met Polly Higgins, a campaigning barrister of enormous energy and vision. She was holding a brief on behalf of the planet, and her life (sadly now deceased) was devoted to persuading nations to stop ecocide. The perspective I had not properly encountered nor understood before was to start treating the planet as a client, on whose behalf you are articulating and advocating for earthly rights, and for freedom from interference. I was so bogged down with the need to have a human client that humanity had passed me by, a kind of existential oversight! Once you start to see ways to protect, to preserve, to improve, you are giving a voice to the natural rumblings around you. Next you need to see whether the existing legal framework copes with the threats.

Polly, therefore, wanted to revive the fifth crime against the peace and security of mankind. To this end, she submitted an amended fresh draft to the UN Law Commission in 2010 containing several elements, the core of which was:

Extensive damage to, destruction of or loss of ecosystems of a given territory, whether by human agency or by any other causes, to such an extent that peaceful enjoyment by the inhabitants of that territory has been or will be severely diminished.

Bit of a mouthful, but definitions are elusive. Corporations, or governments through individuals, can be made personally liable – not only for the cause of the environmental event, but also for failures in a duty of care to mitigate the consequences, even if they did not cause it. You need to read it a few times – at least I did – before the true impact is appreciated.

We both thought it was imperative to ensure the citizen and the public at large could get behind this as well as the people in power. Together with a team of others, lawyers and lay, we thought a mock trial might be the best way of demonstrating what it all meant and how it all might work.

I don't know how she did it, but Polly managed to hire the newly established Supreme Court in Parliament

Square, London, which up until 2009 had been the Middlesex Guildhall. A brilliant coup and backcloth for the first ecocide trial ever, in September 2011!

The undertaking was daunting . . . for me, but not for her. We had to get a judge, counsel, defendants, expert witnesses, a jury, police – and a trial process with charges, or maybe that came first! It was all filmed and is still available on YouTube. I was prosecuting counsel. To say it wasn't exactly my métier would be an understatement, since I had never prosecuted on behalf of the state. However, it gave me a chance to show off my European robes worn in the ICC – elegant and floor length, such that no one cared what you had on underneath!

I was shivering, not because of the robes, but because so much depended on getting this right and making it intelligible.

We based the exercise on two real examples of ecocide. The Deepwater Horizon oil disaster in the Gulf of Mexico, and the Athabasca Tar Sands oil extraction in Alberta, Canada. We indicted two company directors (accomplished actors) who were represented by Christopher Parker KC. He did a mighty fine job at the start of the trial challenging the legitimacy of the charges. If he had won, we would have been up the creek.

Verdicts were returned by the jury of Guilty on the tar sands and Not Guilty on Deepwater. The headlines in the media the next day gave Polly the boost she needed: 'Test Trial Convicts Fossil Fuel Bosses of Ecocide'.

Thereafter, support has been garnered from all corners of the globe, co-ordinated by the Stop Ecocide campaign. An independent panel of jurists has refined the definition. Most recently, in January 2023, the Council of Europe (with 46 member states) has endorsed the demand for ecocide to be a recognised international crime. By February 2023, ten countries, including France and Ukraine, had made it a domestic crime, and twenty-seven more were considering it. It's laborious and time consuming but giving up is not an option. To do so would ratify desecration.

I had the opportunity in 2011 to see exactly that at the tar sands site. I went to lend support to lawyers in Vancouver who were representing the First Nations whose livelihoods and environment were being destroyed by oil extraction, potentially in violation of an agreement with Queen Victoria. It covers an area larger than England where sludgy oil lies beneath Canada's boreal forest. It has been converted into a smell-ridden moonscape, where survival is at stake. The vast wastewater run-off ponds are stagnant and toxic. To prevent birds from even touching down on such a fatal surface, sound cannons are used to deter them.

The First Nations, interestingly, identify their own existence by reference to the earth on which they stand. They are true representatives of the planet.

*

At the other end of the scale is a model of how the people have made all the difference at a local, tangible level. In this case, with the help of the right people in power, the power of the people has been harnessed to bypass disinterest and indolence.

Near where I live, a group of concerned individuals convened an extremely effective version of a People's Inquiry. The scope and object, however, were much more local than previous examples, and were condensed into one manageable and highly pertinent question – What do we need to do in Warwick district to help address climate change by 2030?

Simple and to the point. Exactly what everyone who is bothered wants to know. The outcome of this inquiry is focused on 'action'. Unlike the other examples cited so far, it is not concerned with – equally vital but commonly contentious – issues of fault, responsibility or accountability, which can consume enormous energy and resources. In a sense, it is a specialist People's Inquiry that can constitute an important supplementary component in rejuvenating the jaded nature of democracy we suffer at present.

The local Warwick District Council agreed to fund and sponsor this initiative. An agency, Shared Future CIC, that had experience in this field was commissioned to help establish and oversee its management. Procuring people to take part in such an inquiry must be transparent, fair and proportionate. In criminal trials, the jury is derived from the electoral role for the area covered by a particular court. It is a random selection and attendance is obligatory. On the other hand, the judge and panel for a judicial public inquiry are usually specialists appointed by government. In this instance, the method used involved public announcement and then a random 10,000 invitations sent by postcode, which constituted what was termed the 'lottery' or 'random factor'.

To ensure that the responses reflected a cross-section of the community, a specialist firm was employed to analyze samples by means of an algorithm, to assess diversity and stratification via known demographics of age, gender, ethnicity, disability, location and so on. Unsurprisingly, the result was a larger body than either a normal jury of twelve or a professional panel of four. Provided it is manageable, therein lies its strength.

An important aid to this end was an Oversight/ Advisory panel derived from 13 local interest groups or stakeholders, ranging from Warwick District Council, Warwick University and the National Farmers' Union through to Extinction Rebellion. The hearings were divided into ten sessions, between 12 November 2020 and 4 February 2021. Each one was overseen by an impartial facilitator and was addressed by experts relevant to the issue being considered. The issues chosen started sensibly with basic questions about the nature and causes of climate change, and the science and impact of climate change, then progressed through district carbon emissions, transport, housing, waste and recycling, finance and integration. The jury discussed the evidence presented in each session and ultimately formulated its conclusions.

The recommendations were formidable and far-sighted. As well as educating individual citizens, it has informed and empowered the council to act – in both cases the practicalities related to transport, housing, waste recycling and biodiversity. John and Alix Dearing, both with extensive experience as local councillors, kindly provided a summary for me. 'The council has acted on numerous plans – retro-fitting social and low-income houses; decarbonising council assets; switching council vehicles to electric; divesting fossil fuel investments; negotiating with contractors to reduce their carbon emissions; undertaking a major tree-planting scheme; and rolling out a climate engagement scheme in rural areas.'

The following statement was written by a group of jury members and then edited and discussed by the rest of the jury. Out of the 30 jury members, 27 voted on the recommendations: 21 strongly supported the statement, 3 supported the statement, 2 voted neither to support nor oppose and 1 strongly opposed the statement.

'We are just a group of ordinary people from the Warwick District. We are a diverse group who were randomly selected to join this Climate Change Inquiry. We have different viewpoints but have reached a shared understanding. We now recognise we are in a climate emergency. We must act now, all together and with urgency. Through our conversations with experts and with each other we have come to recognise the importance of immediate action. We are not experts, and we recognise that it may not be 100 per cent possible to implement all our recommendations immediately, however we ask all local organisations and institutions including Warwick District Council to take our recommendations as a mandate to be as ambitious as you can, within the areas we have highlighted, in responding to the emergency that we face. This is everybody's problem; everybody has a role to take action. We are just a small group of people but through our coming together we have become a group bursting with ideas and enthusiasm. We believe that to respond to our emergency the District Council and other organisations must harness the energy and enthusiasm of our people and our communities. We must all make a change for climate change. Your district needs you. We believe the solutions are out there already, we just need to make it happen. If we can't find the examples, then we must be those examples. The District

Council and others must look for every opportunity to influence all who have a role in our district. We must make this happen and the frameworks must be in place to make sure there is accountability (named people) and monitoring (performance indicators) so that everybody can check progress.'

THIS IS AN EMERGENCY.

Now we are talking real business, not just shop. And now the force is with the people and not reliant on the people in power!

Epilogue
The Front Line Today

From the beginning of my work at the Bar, I have been on a learning curve, but not in the usual sense. Not about how to do the job – although I hope I have learned that too – but about the capacity and capabilities of ordinary people against enormous adversity. The origins lie with the wartime and post-war experiences of my parents – steadfast and uncomplaining, despite regular bombing raids, survival risks and then severe austerity and rationing. By comparison, thereafter, I was privileged to have a secure and relatively untroubled peacetime upbringing in a modest suburb of London, attending two reputable local schools.

It's obvious from this, although I had not really thought about it then, that I had a lot to learn. This I learned from the people I represented, all the way through, right up to the present day – not necessarily with every encounter but certainly the ones recounted here. I feel enriched by listening and listening hard. Advocacy for me is not primarily about the art of communication but about compassion.

This opens all sorts of different doors and windows to learn about 'the lives of others' (in the words of the acclaimed film title). The 'others' are the message of this book, not me. It is their example that empowers, and there are more of them on the way. Following are three stories of ordinary citizens on the front line today.

The Forgotten Prisoners

It's 2005. Imagine being told that you need to serve a minimum of one year and nine months in prison, after which you will be eligible for release by the Parole Board into the community. Your crime is attempted robbery – you threatened to punch a shopkeeper unless they handed over the contents of their till. You admit your crime, you know you've done wrong, and this is your punishment. You resign yourself to this time and count the days until you are released back into the community with licence conditions, under the supervision of a probation officer.

Time in prison goes quickly, as every day is the same. The routines are the same. The place is the same. The only changes are the faces of other prisoners who come and go – some are released, others are transferred to other prisons. Soon, one year and nine months is up. The date comes and goes but no one even acknowledges it.

Your children keep asking when you're coming home, but you can't tell them because you have no idea. You start to self-harm and misuse substances in prison to cope. You seek help, but no one – not prison staff, probation officers, lawyers, your MP, the Ministry of Justice – can tell you when you are likely to get out of prison because you were unlucky enough to be one of the 8,700 people who were given the now-defunct sentence of 'imprisonment for public protection' (IPP). With this sentence there's a catch: your minimum term means absolutely nothing.

While this may sound like dystopian fiction, it is real life. Today there are 2,900 people in prison serving these sentences – 95 per cent of them are still in prison more than 10 years after their minimum term. Of those 2,900, 1,400 have never been released. Those who have been released into the community may have been recalled to prison on their licence, often for failing to attend appointments with probation, or for failing a drug test – drug habits which they picked up in prison to try to navigate their way through the sentence.

Fast forward to 2023: your children have grown into adults and have left home. Your wife has divorced you and moved on. Your recollection of life in the community has been reduced to fading and painful memories. The question often asked – both by unsuspecting members of the public and by friends and family members is, 'How is this person still in prison?'. They must have done something much worse than they led us to believe, or they must have committed other crimes in prison.

In 2005, the Criminal Justice Act 2003 introduced a new type of prison sentence called 'imprisonment for public protection'. It sounded great on paper and was sure to be a vote-winner for a government intent on being tough on crime. Prisoners who committed certain types of offences had to be jailed indefinitely and would only be released if they were able to prove to the Parole Board that they were no longer dangerous. They would not be able to sit back in prison and just wait for a release date, they would have to earn it. How would they earn it? By showing that they had used their time in prison to reform.

It was considered at the time to be a good idea and the government envisaged that about a hundred people a year would be sentenced under this regime. It became apparent within a couple of years that this was not the case – the real number was more like 1,000 every year. By the time IPP sentences were abolished, there were 8,700 people serving these sentences. After abolition, judges could no longer give out any new IPP sentences, but the law was not retrospective, which is why there are still thousands of people stuck in prison today.

If you are sentenced to imprisonment for public protection, the only way you can get out of prison is to prove to the Parole Board that you are not a danger to anyone any more. The best way, in theory at least, is to admit your guilt (tough for those who are appealing) and enrol on a course in prison with other offenders, after which psychologists will write reports about you and decide whether you are still 'dangerous'. The only problem is that the course waiting list is three years long. In the meantime, you've lost your home, your relationship and you barely see your family any more.

After the abolition of the sentence in 2012, and despite the practice being branded 'a stain on the system', the government has failed to tackle the problem. Even the IPP sentence's creator, Lord Blunkett, has publicly declared that it is a continued injustice which he deeply regrets. Apart from, of course, ensuring that there are no future victims of this inhumane sentence, very little has been done to ameliorate the awful position that those already subject to the sentence find themselves in.

The Justice Select Committee (JSC) launched an inquiry into the IPP sentence and concluded at the end of 2022 that, among other things, the fairest way to deal with the continuing problem of IPP prisoners would be to re-sentence them. The absence of hope, and lack of control over when or if they are going to be released, has often seriously damaged or destroyed the mental health of these people. Some have been sent to secure psychiatric wards for treatment, others have simply given up hope and – unsurprisingly – a significantly higher percentage of IPP prisoners than other prisoners have committed suicide. In February 2023, within days of the government announcing that it would not be acting on the JSC's recommendation to re-sentence IPP prisoners, three more of them took their own lives.

Campaigners, who are often friends and families of those incarcerated under this inhuman regime, have rigorously pressed for reform. Donna Mooney's brother committed suicide while serving IPP. She has since campaigned for IPP prisoners and set up UNGRIPP for this purpose. 'When someone you love dies in custody, in the circumstances that my brother died [in], you are faced with an indescribable and unmeasurable pain,' she explained. 'Pain that paralyses you for months and years. You are changed in a way that you can never return to. A before and after. It's a pain that nobody should ever have to live with. So I began campaigning to try to stop the deaths so that people would not have to go through what my brother went through, the torment he lived with and to stop people from experiencing the pain that I am now faced with every day.'

Donna's situation is different from most other families of IPP prisoners. She continued, 'Most people haven't lost someone. When my brother died and I got all the information following his very traumatic inquest, I watched the video of him being restrained. In those moments I felt very angry at what had been done to him and I had no power to change that. The inquest happened and there was no acknowledgement at all what the sentence had done to him, which fuelled my anger and frustration. The things that led to me campaigning were the anger – I wanted to channel it into something positive – I wanted some accountability for what this is doing to people, and for my brother not to become a statistic. These are people, and they count for something. The realisation is how terrible this process is, and that it has to stop. To some degree I now have nothing to lose – my brother is dead, he can't be recalled if I'm too vocal.'

Shirley Debono's son Shaun Lloyd was given an IPP sentence. He was just 18 and his crime was street robbery of a mobile phone. After some initial confusion, in which Shaun was mistakenly given a life sentence, the sentence was amended to IPP. A governor in the prison told him that he was never getting out of prison and would die in prison. When the IPP sentence was introduced, Shirley – like many others, including prison staff – had no idea what the sentence meant, either in practical or in legal terms. 'Even then when it was rectified to an IPP sentence, I thought it was a rehabilitation course. When I realised that it was a life sentence, I had a breakdown. I smashed all the dishes in my kitchen, I was screaming, "I want my son back".'

Shirley was determined to do something about it. She set up a Free Shaun Lloyd website, and arranged a protest outside Cardiff prison, which was covered by local press in Wales. The community became involved. That was the start of her campaign.

Despite having parole hearings every couple of years, Shaun was unable to persuade the Parole Board that it was not necessary for the protection of the public (the legal test for release) that he should remain in custody. This was perplexing, given that the reports prepared about him for the purpose of his parole were positive and the staff were saying nice things about him. On his eighth year inside prison, and after another parole refusal, Shirley went to visit Shaun. 'I miss you, Mum', he'd said, with tears running down his cheeks. It wasn't until much later that Shaun confided to her that he had been planning to take his own life that night. He had lost all hope of ever getting released.

Shaun was eventually released from prison but IPP prisoners are on indefinite licence – and therefore liable to be recalled to prison at any time – and he has been recalled on numerous occasions. On one occasion, knowing that he faced further time in prison, he absconded from an open prison with no shoes on, wearing just a pair of tracksuit bottoms and a T-shirt. Shirley explained, 'His head was gone, he didn't want to go back to prison indefinitely.'

At the time of writing, there are 1,498 IPP prisoners currently in custody after being recalled. Donna said, 'Ultimately my goal is for people to be re-sentenced. Despite it taking a long time, people would know that there is an end goal at some point.'

As George Monbiot recently wrote in the *Guardian*, 'A great wrong has been done. Almost everyone in power accepts it is wrong, but none are prepared to address it.'

Smart Motorways

On the morning of 7 June 2019, Jason Mercer (44) and Alexandru Murgeanu (22) pulled over near Junction 34 of the M1 Northbound, following a minor collision between their vehicles. That particular section of the M1 motorway is a Smart Motorway – which means that all lanes were running, and the previous hard shoulder had been converted into a permanent live lane. With no lay-by for almost a mile, Jason and Alexandru both parked against the barrier, on what would have been the hard shoulder, in order to exchange insurance details as required by law. The safety features that were supposed to have been in place to monitor this kind of activity on the motorway and close the lane did not detect them, even though the two men were there for more than ten minutes. The live lane on that stretch of the M1 was only closed after they had both been crushed to death by a heavy goods vehicle.

Claire Mercer is instantly recognisable by her fuchsia hair. She appears regularly on television and has done for the last four years, nearly always from her kitchen. Her dog, a rescue from Romania, is curled up in a chair in the next room. 'I went and identified Jason,' she told me. 'There was a blanket over his body but I touched him, I thought that's what they do, they put a cage in place. I went straight into campaign mode, because I couldn't cope. I've had several breakdowns since then. It's absolutely shattered me as a person. Four years later, in some ways I feel that I've gone back to being like that. Other times I break, just the slightest thing sends me into a full nervous breakdown. I did 36 interviews back-to-back one day – and then the slightest thing will break me. At first it was lonely, I would be sobbing in bed, the pillow wet. Lying in a super king bed all alone. I only had two modes at first: working and campaigning, or grieving.'

She has campaigned tirelessly for the removal of all Smart Motorways since Jason's death. Recently the government announced that there would be no 'new' Smart Motorways, which attracted a lot of press. 'I had a warning that it was coming,' she explained. 'They announced it at 6pm on Sunday evening. Everyone thought the headline meant something that it didn't – it was only no NEW Smart Motorways. It wasn't even worth the announcement. They are basically scrapping about four schemes. Half of the others are already dynamic – All Lane Running – so that never has a hard shoulder. Several are opening without the hard shoulder because they're substantially completed.'

The campaign has taken its toll on Claire. 'Having to repeat that for four days, it really got to me. I became very mechanical. Talking about my husband being hit by an HGV. I'm talking about two people being smashed by a 40-ton truck.' Having become a very vocal and visible campaigner, she has often sat down with the people in power. 'They don't know how to cope with it. They've tried a few different tactics – friending me, ignoring me. Nick Harris, Chief Executive of National Highways, suddenly invited me to a meeting. I said yes, even though we had been in litigation for two years. At 9.30pm the night before, he sent me an email saying his lawyers had advised he wasn't able to meet with me.'

She is adamant that she won't stop until the hard shoulder has been restored on all motorways. 'I'm going to keep going; what's going to stop me? Fucking stubbornness – that's what you need.'

The Legacy of Orgreave

The 18 June 2024 will mark the 40th anniversary of the battle for Orgreave. There will be those reading this who were not born at the time, and others who may never have heard of this event. I have referred to it earlier in the book (see page 137), but it has a significance well beyond its years. It concerns what should be a fundamental quality of our parliamentary democracy – the right to protest and make the voice of the citizen heard. It is constantly paraded by those about to restrict it.

The facts of Orgreave are incontrovertible. As part of a year-long strike, a group of miners attended a picket of the Orgreave coking plant to dissuade deliveries. The police employed new public order tactics to kettle, or corral, the miners into a confined space, where they sustained serious head and other injuries from the uncontrolled use of truncheons by police on foot and horseback.

Mass arrests were being carried out as policy (11,000 in total throughout the strike), and a raft of serious charges were prepared against the miners. The gravest of all was riot, which would have attracted an immediate deterrent prison sentence for those convicted.

When this pre-prepared travesty came to trial a year later, the whole prosecution case collapsed abruptly and catastrophically amid the revelations that officers had lied, fabricated evidence and forged documents. The final straw was a police witness who excused himself from attendance on the basis of a note he submitted, claiming he had become sick at the sight of Orgreave!

As part of a team of lawyers defending the miners, I had the good fortune to be provided with first-class evidence of police malpractice – caught out by their own police video of the day, by miners who had cameras and filmed what really happened on the ground, and by courageous independent observers who did the same.

Despite this compelling material, not a single police officer was prosecuted for perjury, for causing grievous bodily harm, or for assault. Nor was a single police officer even disciplined for such behaviour. It was as if they had been granted some form of unspoken immunity. In other words, there has never been any accountability for the original unlawful use of force nor the co-ordinated cover-up. Repeated requests for an inquiry have been routinely rejected.

You do not have to look far to ascertain why. The conduct of police throughout the strike, but especially at Orgreave, was not just some operational decision on the ground. It was a political planned response by a Conservative government bent on silencing the 'enemy within', as Prime Minister Margaret Thatcher characterised the miners. It was planned and orchestrated. Coal had been stockpiled to outlast a strike of this proportion. The tactics employed had been devised by senior police, including the one in charge at Orgreave, and set out in a Public Order Manual that had been kept secret. I managed to expose its existence during cross-examination.

An inquiry was rejected at the start because it would have uncovered the politicisation of the police and how public protest was to be handled from then on.

Such tactics surfaced again during the printworkers' dispute (1986–87 in Wapping), which I attended as a legal observer, during the poll tax protest in 1990, during the G20 protests in 2009, and during the student fees and grants protests in 2010. There was particularly dangerous corralling in Parliament Square and on Waterloo Bridge during the last of these.

The essential issue in all of this is the diminution and erosion of the basic right to protest. There has been a succession of ever-more draconian proposals to increase police powers and put stringent limits on protest, including electronic tagging and injunctions. The survival of this right is a vital outlet for citizens who wish to advance change in the public interest. Arrests at the coronation in 2023 are symptomatic of where we are at present. As Charles Walker MP* quite rightly pointed out, freedom to protest notionally persists, but not the right. Without

---

* Charles Walker, the Conservative MP for Broxbourne.

the right, the freedom means little and becomes an empty gesture to be invoked regularly by those reducing its ambit. A right is an entitlement – moral and legal – imbued with the characteristic of inalienability. That's why the conventions and treaties speak of rights first and foremost. Otherwise, the freedoms risk becoming illusory. And that's why the people who cherish these rights are now branded as examples of 'woke' and have become the new 'enemy within' for the people in temporary power.

The proposals have led to a panoply of legislation enacted to curtail the voice of the people in the same manner as the Restoration Parliament treated the Quakers, the most recent rushed through days before the coronation in 2023. On top of the older offences of riot and unlawful assembly, a huge range of public order offences has been added. The cherished right of peaceful protest has been steadily eroded by a plethora of legal restraints and preconditions, violations of which constitute further offences in themselves. The nadir was reached in 2022 with proposals (defeated twice in the House of Lords) to even cap noise levels.

It will surprise no one, therefore, that this steady decline in respect for basic rights and the rule of law – both in policy and practice – by successive governments has placed the UK on a slope that ends dangerously close to a regime akin to those in Belarus, North Korea, Afghanistan, China and

Russia, regimes that brook no opposition. In March 2023, Civicus Monitor, the annual global index of civil society and civic freedoms, downgraded the UK to 'increasingly authoritarian' and 'a hostile environment'. The latter words are strikingly familiar, having been uttered in 2012 by a British Prime Minister seeking to promote exactly that as a deterrent to those with aspirations of becoming British citizens!

Last Words

While the very last words of this book were being written, no better illustration of its *raison d'être* could have been provided than the desperate antics of the people in power. All of a sudden, ex-Prime Minister Boris Johnson has resigned from Parliament. This he has done in order to avoid facing, in person, a debate about his misconduct in the core institution of our democracy, the House of Commons.

The House was debating whether to accept the findings of a damning report by the Privileges Committee that found Mr Johnson had misled Parliament about lockdown parties, which took place while social distancing measures were being adhered to by the people of the country. It has to be remembered that the Privileges Committee, its remit and its chair, were all approved by Parliament itself. For it to be ignored, let alone abused, by the ex-PM and his lobby is another indication of the culture of contempt for the rule of law and the interests of the people that runs just below the surface of power.

Although 354 members supported the committee's report and 7 voted against, that still leaves 289 MPs who did not bother to turn up or chose not to vote. One of those is the serving Prime Minister Rishi Sunak. Not present and nothing to say – a repeat of the memorial to mark the 30th anniversary of the death of Stephen Lawrence.

But it wasn't just the House of Commons Mr Johnson was unable to face. Far more significantly, it was also his own constituency. Stepping down from his role of MP with immediate effect. What courtesies were paid to the people I wonder? Little or none.

There is only one way out of this continuing debacle of crazed power brokers. It is for citizens to assert their own skills and consciences in the interest of justice for all – planet included. To lead by example, rather than be led by the myopic self-interest of personal aggrandisement and accumulation of wealth.

Time for change
And the change is you
Silence is no longer an option.

Endnotes

1. Interim Report, Chapter 33, Paragraph 33.6.
2. Interim Report, Volume 4, Paragraph 34.13.
3. Universal Declaration of Human Rights (1948), Article 25.
4. The Charter of the UN (1945), Article 1.
5. International Covenant on Economic, Social and Cultural Rights (1966), Article 12 (1) and (2).
6. Attorney General's Reference No.3 of 2003.

Acknowledgements

Special thanks to Lorna Hackett at Hackett and Dabbs, assisted by Emily Hayward. Thanks also to John Azah at the Kingston Race and Equalities Council, Danielle Fahiya at BBC Wales, and Alix and John Dearing, councillors in Warwickshire.

And to all the interviewees: Lawrence Dallaglio, Shirley Debono, Jenni Hicks, Neville Lawrence, Donna Mooney, Lynette, partner of the late Mahmood Mattan, Claire Mercer and Sukhdev Reel.

This **monoray** book was crafted and published by Jake Lingwood, Leanne Bryan, Joanna Smith, Mel Four, Anthony Burrill, Jouve and Allison Gonsalves.